WHAT OTHERS ARE S

Lies Girls Believe is a fantastic t
stand strong against the lies th
and twenties and beyond. Inves
with Truth. Because the old saying got it right—an ounce of prevention is *definitely* worth a pound of cure!

MARY A. KASSIAN
Author of *Girls Gone Wise*

I loved *Lies Young Women Believe* by Nancy DeMoss Wolgemuth and Dannah Gresh. And now, I am so excited to see *Lies Girls Believe* introduce younger girls to the Truth that sets them free. Only Jesus can do that, but Dannah makes understanding how to experience it so accessible. I can't wait to get it into the hands of my granddaughters!

CATHE LAURIE
Founder and director of Virtue, the women's ministry at
Harvest Christian Fellowship

Our daughters are being surrounded by positive sounding messages like "Girl Boss" and "Girls Rule the World." But is that the Truth? No—the Truth is that *Jesus* is the boss and He rules! I'm so glad Dannah Gresh has written this guide for moms to combat the lies of social media, pop culture, and foolish friends. Grab your daughter and this book, and head to a favorite spot to talk. I know this book will be the conversation starter for many intentional dates with my daughters!

ARLENE PELLICANE
Speaker and author of *Parents Rising* and *31 Days to Becoming a Happy Mom*

Girls have never had a more fun way to discover Truth and help them recognize the lies that break trust and relationships. Dannah Gresh clearly compares the lies to Truth in ways girls can identify to correct beliefs about themselves and discover Christ's goal for their life.

RON HUNTER JR.
Cofounder and director of the D6 Conference
Author of *DNA of D6: Building Blocks of Generational Discipleship*

Our girls' lives depend on their mothers knowing God's Truth. That sounds like a cliché, but for me it was and is still paramount to saving my daughter's life. Dannah unfolds a process that sets the mother-daughter team free to dispel lies and uncover the Truth God wants us to believe about His love for us, our families, friendships, and our future. You'll learn how to listen, dwell, believe, and act on God's Truth. Therein is freedom.

JENNY SUMMERS

Executive Director of Pregnancy Resource Clinic and mother of eight

Lies
GIRLS
Believe
& THE TRUTH THAT SETS THEM FREE

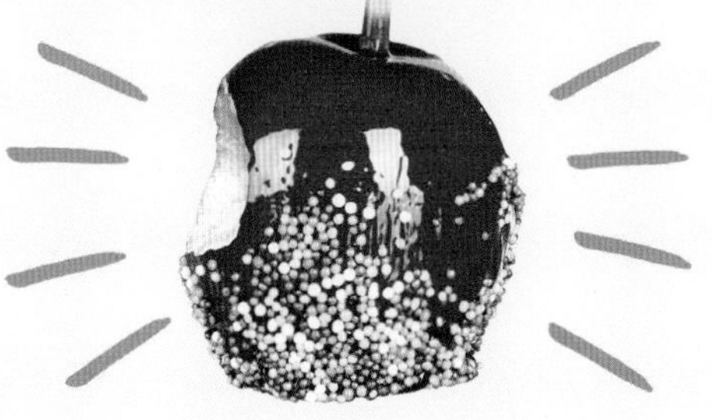

BY **DANNAH GRESH**

AND

(Write your name here!)

NANCY DeMOSS WOLGEMUTH

LIES WE BELIEVE SERIES EDITOR

MOODY PUBLISHERS
CHICAGO

All emphasis in Scripture has been added.

Some names and details have been changed to protect the privacy of individuals.

Edited by Ashleigh Slater
Lies We Believe Series Editor: Nancy DeMoss Wolgemuth
Interior Design & Ilustrations: Julia Ryan/www.DesignByJulia
Cover Design: Faceout Studio
Cover Image: Cover photo of candy apple copyright © 2018 Yastremska/Bigstock (200730625). All rights reserved.
Photo Credits: © Jason Nelson p55; © Douglas Saum p79

Library of Congress Cataloging-in-Publication Data

Names: Gresh, Dannah, 1967- author.
Title: Lies girls believe : and the truth that sets them free / by Dannah Gresh.
Description: Chicago : Moody Publishers, 2019.
Identifiers: LCCN 2018049377 (print) | LCCN 2019004291 (ebook) | ISBN 9780802494016 (ebook) | ISBN 9780802414472
Subjects: LCSH: Preteen girls--Religious life--Juvenile literature. | Truthfulness and falsehood--Religious aspects--Christianity--Juvenile literature.
Classification: LCC BV4551.3 (ebook) | LCC BV4551.3 .G734 2019 (print) | DDC 248.8/33--dc23
LC record available at https://lccn.loc.gov/2018049377

ISBN: 978-0-8024-1447-2

Printed by: Versa Press in East Peoria, IL, March 2019

We hope you enjoy this book from Moody Publishers. Our goal is to provide high-quality, thought-provoking books and products that connect truth to your real needs and challenges. For more information on other books and products written and produced from a biblical perspective, go to www.moodypublishers.com or write to:

Moody Publishers
820 N. LaSalle Boulevard
Chicago, IL 60610

3 5 7 9 10 8 6 4 2

Printed in the United States of America

A NOTE FOR MOMS

I'm overjoyed to have your trust as you give this book to your daughter. It will be most effective if you use the companion, *A Mom's Guide to Lies Girls Believe*, along with it.

Some of the lies today's tween girls face are on topics you and I didn't even know about until we were teenagers or adults. This book navigates some challenging subjects, such as becoming a woman, using social media, and embracing God's design for marriage, motherhood, and two genders: male and female.

A team of about ten moms, grandmas, and spiritual mothers helped me carefully and prayerfully write and edit this content. We also asked many other mothers to review it. We concur that most girls between the ages of 9–12 are ready for and need this book. However, ultimately, God has entrusted you with the responsibility to determine when your daughter is ready for any given conversation.

Please take time to read the table of contents and preview any chapters you may have questions about before sharing this book with your daughter or perhaps other tween girls in your life. Though we have taken care to write every word in a prayerful, sensitive, and biblical manner, there may be conversations you want to have with your daughter before she reads the book on her own. I'm praying for you and your tween daughter as you journey together through *Lies Girls Believe*!

Dannah

CONTENTS

PART 3: THE TRUTH THAT SETS YOU FREE

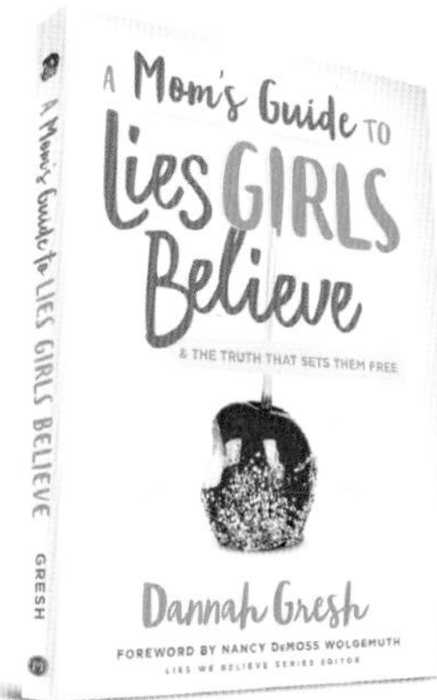

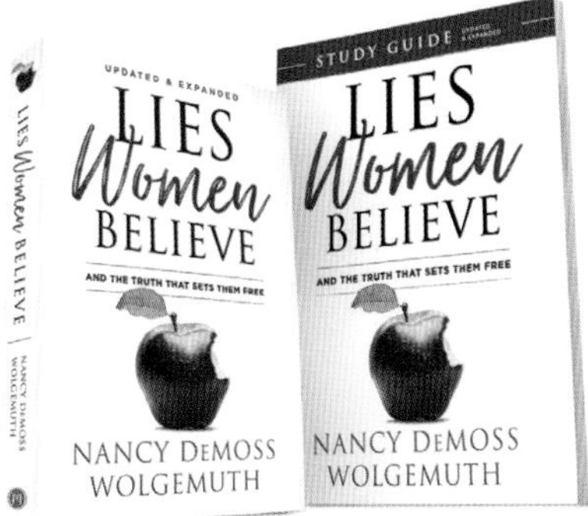

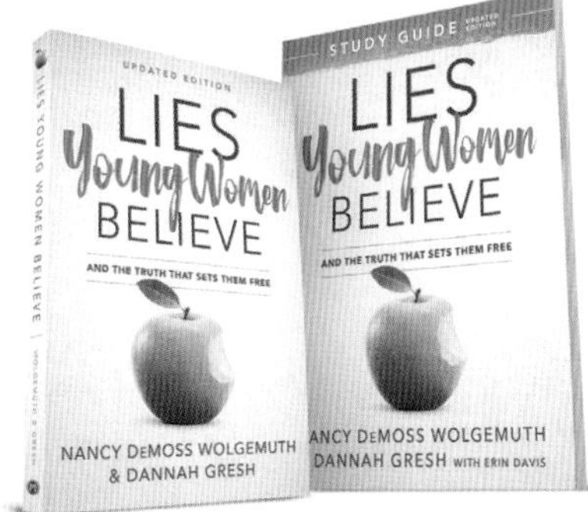

This book is one of several on the topic of lies we believe and the truth that sets us free. Together, they have been used by God to help set one and a half million people free!

You could be next! This wonderful collection of books was the idea of Nancy DeMoss Wolgemuth. She is the Lies We Believe Series Editor of this book, and the one I wrote for your mom titled *A Mom's Guide to Lies Girls Believe.* I hope your mom can read it while you enjoy this one. She might also really like the first book in the series, *Lies Women Believe.*

Be sure to tell her!

Dannah wrote this book with a lot of help. The names of those people are in *A Mom's Guide to Lies Girls Believe* because they helped with that one, too. But it just has to be mentioned that this one was written in beautiful Samana, Dominican Republic, at the house of Rosalia and Marcial Najri, where Bob and Dannah were hosted by Hector and Maria Vilorio.

Introduction

Have Your Feelings Ever Confused You?

HI, I'M DANNAH!

A few years ago, I was super **freaked out** about the problems tween girls face. **Mean girls. Frenemies.** Social media. **BOY CRAZINESS. Fashion. BEAUTY. Report cards.** It seemed like a lot of girls needed help, so I've been writing books ever since.

I'd also like to introduce you to my friend, **NANCY.** ▶ She wrote a book called *Lies Women Believe and the Truth That Sets Them Free.* It was a really good idea, and an important book that helped a lot of your moms and grandmas solve problems they had in their lives. It made me want to write this book just for you.

HOWEVER, there's another important person who is going to write this book. **YOU**.

GRAB SOME FUN COLORED PENCILS OR PENS.

You're about to need them.

Turn to page 5. There's a place for you to write the name of my coauthor for this book: **YOU**. **Write your name there now.**

Welcome to the team!

Let's solve some problems together.

GIRL DRAMA QUIZ

Many girls write to me about their problems. They use some of the words below to describe how they **feel**. **Circle one of the options in each set of words to describe how you feel MOST OFTEN**!

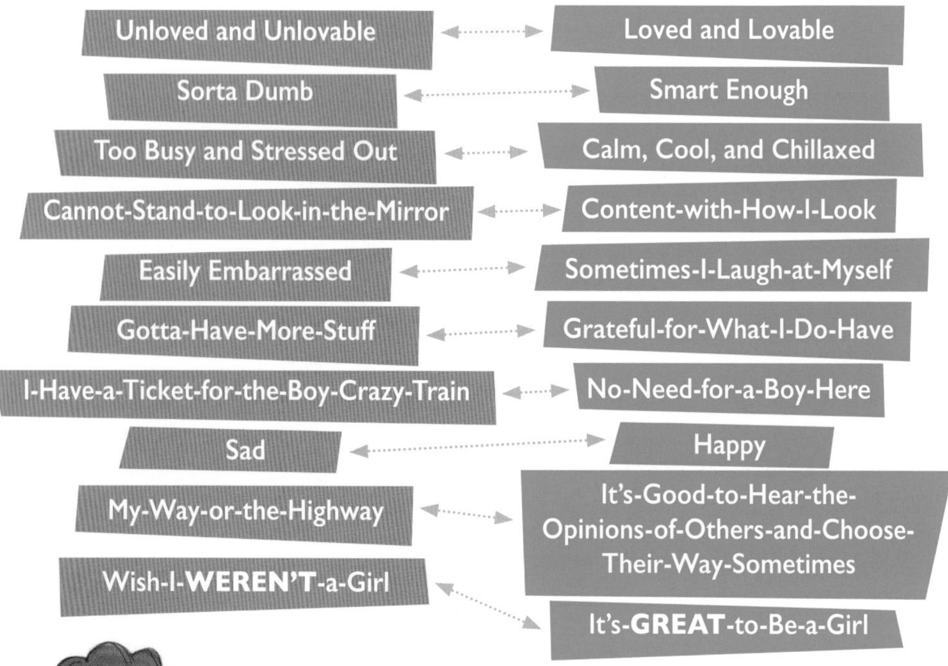

If you circled any of the yucky feelings on the left, you're not alone! The week I began writing this book, a beautiful 12-year-old girl named Sadie* came up to me. She had bright eyes, clear, brown skin, and black, curly hair. But a tear slipped down her cheek as she said:

"Can you help me? I feel so embarrassed about the way I look. My arms are hairy compared to other girls', and sometimes kids at school even tell me I should shave them!"

Those students were being mean! The hair on her arms didn't look bad at all, but she had started to think about it **all the time**, **EVERY DAY**. It made her believe she was ugly. When in fact, she wasn't!

* Sadie is not my friend's real name, but she is a real friend. Throughout this book, I'm going to use real stories—NOT FICTION—about real girls, but most of the time I don't use their real names.

She had begun to believe a lie.

If you circled anything on the left side, **you** may have the same problem as Sadie.

YOU HAVE BEEN LIED TO.

It feels bad to be lied to. But did you know that lies make us feel bad **even when we don't know we've been lied to**? My friend **FELT** ugly, but didn't know it was a lie. She thought it was the truth!

It's normal to feel sad, ugly, lonely, stupid, weird, and all kinds of other bad things sometimes. But when feelings stick to us **all the time**, **EVERY DAY**, that's not good. I call those feelings that never go away "sticky" feelings.

Satan wants you to feel bad. If you circled any of the words on the left side of my quiz, you are experiencing something Satan has planned. He wants to steal joy, peace, and other good stuff from you.

But Jesus wants something entirely different for you. Check out this Bible verse. It tells us something Jesus said to His followers. He wants us to know and understand it too.

TRUTH NUGGET:
"[Satan]'s purpose is to steal and kill and destroy; My purpose is to give [you] a rich and satisfying life." (John 10:10 NLT)

Understanding "Sticky" Feelings

When you accidentally touch a hot pot and it burns you, your skin tells you, "Don't do that!" Or when you touch a soft, comfy blanket, your skin says, "Yes, do that!" It helps you know what is safe and unsafe for your body. Your feelings, or emotions, are kind of like the skin of your heart. (The inside part of you that has feelings, not the organ that pumps blood.)

In a similar way, your feelings can protect your heart. When it is under God's control and you use God's Truth to direct and respond to your feelings, they are good tools from God.

For example, when you start to hang out with a friend who lies a lot, your feelings tell you, "This feels bad! Back away from this person." When you find a friend who is faithful, your feelings say, "Yes, this feels good! Hang out with her more!" Your feelings help you to know what is safe and what is unsafe for your heart.

One important sign that your feelings are working the way they should is that they come and go. They do their job, and then they wait until you need them again. They aren't "sticky." You don't feel them **all the time**, **EVERY DAY**.

God created both good **and** bad feelings, and they can both be useful if you use God's Truth to respond to them. But when you have a bad feeling and you don't know **why**, or it just never goes away and you feel it all the time, **EVERY DAY**, that's a "sticky" feeling. It may be evidence that you believe a lie!

If you mostly circled words on the right side of my quiz, you are experiencing what Jesus has planned for you: a good and **satisfying** life!

Which side of the list describes how you feel **MOST OF THE TIME**? (You can figure this out by comparing which one has more circled words.) **Write your answer below:**

Notes from Nancy will occasionally appear in the pages of this book. These are things Nancy has either said to me as she encouraged me to write this book for you, or stuff she wrote in *Lies Women Believe*.

The James 5 Challenge

A long time ago, I was reading my Bible when two Bible verses[1] seemed to jump right off the page at me. They tell me (and you) to be careful to notice when someone starts to "wander away from the Truth," and to help save each other from believing lies.

These verses were God's challenge that led me to write *Lies Women Believe* for your moms and grandmas. I hope they will also challenge you. We need each other to help us know the difference between the Truth and a lie because our feelings can confuse us.

No matter what, this book is for you!

The whole girl world tends to get stuck in their feelings and believe lies **sometimes.** If you have a lot of bad feelings, this book will help you find the Truth that leads you to satisfaction. If you tend to feel good most of the time, this book will help you stay there.

Ready? Let's Get Started!

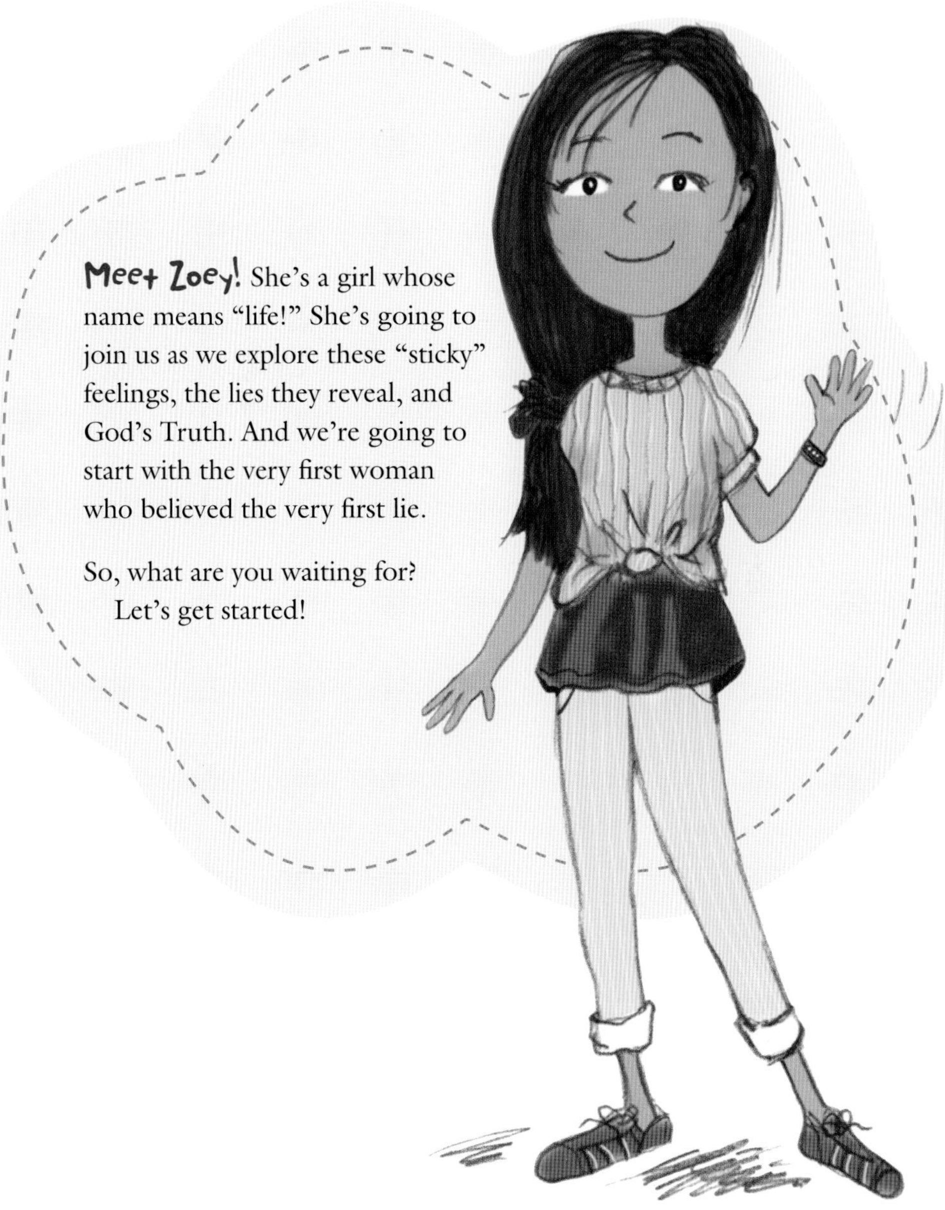

Meet Zoey! She's a girl whose name means "life!" She's going to join us as we explore these "sticky" feelings, the lies they reveal, and God's Truth. And we're going to start with the very first woman who believed the very first lie.

So, what are you waiting for?
Let's get started!

Truth ...or Problems!

CHAPTER 1

A Snake Told the First Lie

(Where do lies come from?)

So . . . some of my friends have the latest social media apps on their devices, but my parents say I don't need them. But . . . I **do** have my own tablet. I **could** download one, but I dunno. Should I? I mean, I have a friend who did it without telling her parents . . . AND **they still don't know!** Would it be a lie if I do it, and just don't tell them?

Zoey has a problem! If she downloads an app her parents have clearly told her she can't have, she would only create more problems. She would be **LIVING a lie** even if she is not **TELLING a lie**. Anytime we intend to deceive someone, we are lying.

Today, we'll discover just how many problems our "sticky" feelings can get us into, if we let them make us believe lies! Grab your colored pencils. It's time to start our study and meet Adam and Eve—and a snake.

LIE

"a false statement with intent to deceive; an inaccurate statement"[2]

A SNAKE TOLD THE FIRST LIE

Read these Bible verses now, and then I'll help you mark them up to study.

The serpent was the shrewdest of all the

wild animals the LORD God had made. One

day he asked the woman, "Did God really

say you must not eat the fruit from any trees

in the garden?"

"Of course we may eat fruit from the trees in

the garden," the woman replied. "It's only the

fruit from the tree in the of the garden that we

are not allowed to eat. God said, 'You must not eat it or even touch it; if you do, you will die.' "

"You won't die!" the serpent replied to the woman. "God knows that your eyes will be opened as soon as you eat it, and you will be like God, knowing both good and evil."

The woman was convinced. She saw that the tree was beautiful and its fruit looked delicious, and she wanted the wisdom it would give her. So she took some of the fruit and ate it. Then she gave to her husband, who was with her, and he ate it, too. At that moment their eyes were opened, and they suddenly felt shame at their nakedness. So they sewed fig leaves together to cover themselves. (Genesis 3:1–7)

THE WOMAN BELIEVED THE LIE

The first lie wasn't told by just any old snake. This serpent was Satan, or the devil, in disguise. The Bible tells us that he is the "father of lies."

TRUTH NUGGET: "The devil . . . was a murderer from the beginning. He has always hated the truth, because there is no truth in him. When he lies, it is consistent with his character; for he is a liar and the father of lies." (John 8:44 NLT)

He told this first lie to the first woman who ever lived, Eve. But Satan wasn't the only one participating in the lie. **Eve listened to the lie**.

Use a RED pencil to double underline the FIRST sentence above where the snake told the FIRST lie. We've already underlined it once for you. Just add the second line.

The first lie was a half-truth. God had told Adam there was **just one tree** in the garden they could not eat from, but **alllllll the rest** were a feast for them. Yet Satan tried to make Eve **FEEL** like God said they couldn't eat **any** of the fruit!

Eve should have stopped talking to that lying snake right away! But she didn't. Instead, **Eve began to dwell on the lie**. Dwelling is kind of like when we have "sticky" feelings and we think about something **all the time**, **EVERY DAY**.

Grab your ORANGE pencil and double underline the first words Eve says to the snake, beginning with: "Of course we may eat fruit from the trees in the garden. . ."

Eve's dwelling turned to explaining. She knew what the snake said wasn't quite true. But she tried to explain things, and got herself into big trouble! That's when the snake went for the big lie: **"You won't die!"**

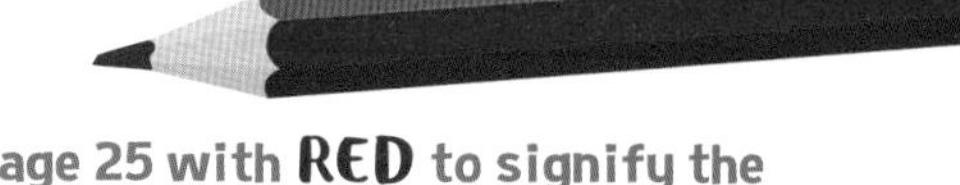

Double underline that sentence on page 25 with RED to signify the snake's words. This was the second time he lied to Eve. It's also when Eve's emotions began to take control.

Maybe she **FELT** confused.

"Wait . . . did Adam misunderstand what God told him?!"

Or maybe she **FELT** rebellious.

"If that's how God is going to be, I don't *want* to follow God's rules!"

Or maybe she **FELT** afraid.

"Oh no! What if God isn't as good as we think He is?"

We don't know what Eve was thinking or feeling, but we can see that she allowed her feelings to be in control. That's when something really bad happened: **Eve began to believe the lie**. She questioned God's Truth!

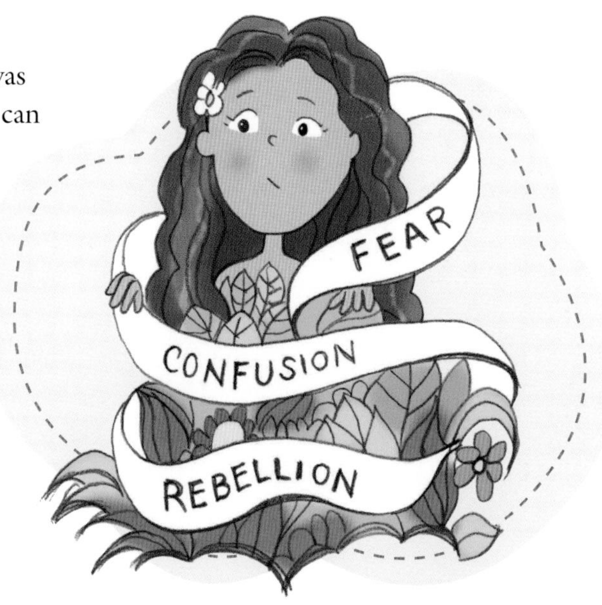

Go to page 25 again. Grab your PURPLE pencil and double underline the words that tell us that Eve was beginning to believe the lie. They are:

"The woman was convinced. She saw that the tree was beautiful and its fruit looked delicious, and she wanted the wisdom . . ."

God knew that Adam and Eve would die if they ate the fruit, and He wanted to protect them. That's why He told them not to eat it.

Did you know that Satan is still lying to us today? He does not disguise himself as a snake anymore, but he still gets dressed up so we can't recognize him. Here are some of the different costumes he wears:

- **Commercials and ads** that tell us we'll be more beautiful if we just buy this pair of jeans or that brand of lip gloss.
- **Friends** who try to convince us to do things our parents don't want us to do, like watch a movie we aren't supposed to see.
- **Teachers or coaches** that seem like they know a lot, but disagree with what the Bible teaches.
- **Our desires** that tell us we need a certain relationship to be happy, like a popular friend or a boyfriend.
- **Our culture** that tells us crazy stuff, like we MUST have social media to have friends.

Oh, that reminds me of Zoey! I wonder what she will decide about downloading that app onto her tablet. Just like God had rules about the trees in the garden, Zoey's parents have rules about social media.

Wanna know what I think?

I think Zoey's parents are pretty smart!

Most social media apps offer a suggested age for use—usually 13, but sometimes 17 or older. Why? Because those apps can do crazy stuff to our feelings! They can cause a lot of "sticky" feelings that make girls feel sad, ugly, stressed, and have **F**ear **O**f **M**issing **O**ut or **FOMO**.[3]

Do you think Zoey should download the app? As her friend, what would you say to her? **Write your ideas below.**

Let's find out what Zoey decides in the next chapter!

A Woman Wanted Some Fruit

(Where do lies get their power?)

I did it. I can't believe it, but I did it. I downloaded the app and my parents don't have a clue! I can chat with my friends anytime I want now. I stayed up late last night doing it. I finally have a life!

Oh, Zoey! I was hoping you would not make that decision. You just disobeyed your parents **BIG TIME**! And the creators of the social media apps themselves would tell you that you are too young! Sure, it feels good to be able to connect to your friends, but you're going to be in trouble real soon. You have acted a lot like Eve did when the snake lied to her. Let's go back to Genesis to ask an important question!

WHAT DID SATAN WANT EVE TO DO?

When Satan told the first life, his goal was for Eve to **act** on the lie.

Grab a GREEN pencil. Now look at Genesis 3:1-7 on page 25 again. Double underline the words:

"So she took some of the fruit and ate it. Then she gave some to her husband, who was with her, and he ate it, too."

Circle every time the word ate is used.

Okay, fill in these blanks:

Satan was trying to get Eve to __________

a piece of fruit that God had told her not to __________ .*

Sadly, Eve ate the fruit. (So did Adam!) **Eve acted on the lie**. She sinned by doing something that was against God's rules.

To this day, Satan continues to lie to us with one goal in mind: to get us to take action. He wants us to sin.

SIN

doing what is wrong or not doing what is right according to God's rules

(1 John 3:4)

* The answer to both of these blanks is **EAT**!

This brings us to something important: lies have no power **without our help**. Eve **chose** to cooperate with Satan in four ways.

HOW EVE COOPERATED WITH SATAN

1. She **listened** to Satan's lies.
2. She **dwelled** on Satan's lies.
3. She **believed** Satan's lies.
4. She **acted** on Satan's lies.

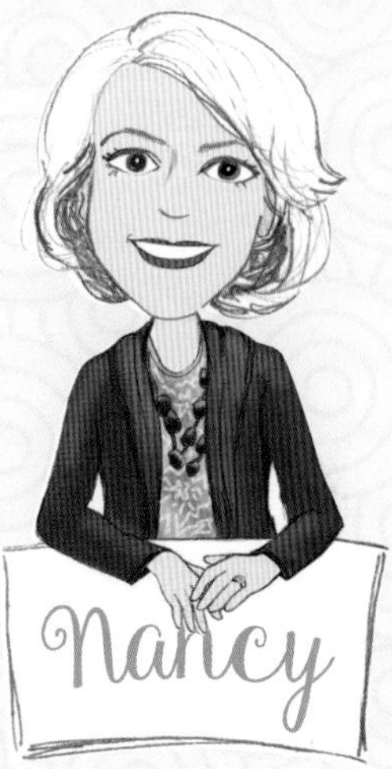

Let's clearly note these four ways as we study. We will look at Eve's situation again, and consider how we do the very same thing she did to cooperate with lies.

1

We cooperate by listening to lies.

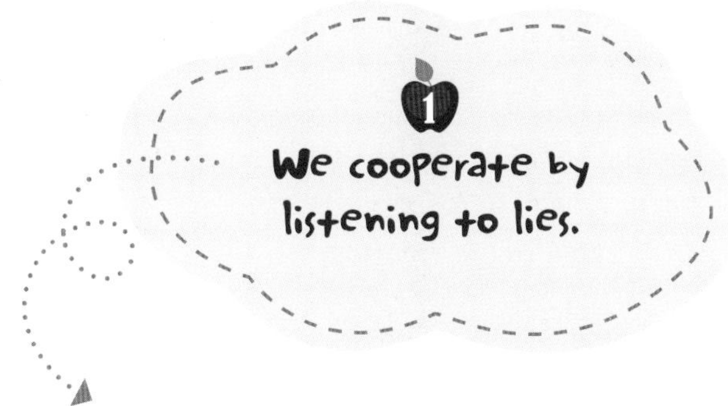

The first mistake Eve made was getting close enough to the snake to listen to the lie. She never should have been hanging out near that tree!

Grab your **RED** pencil and go to page 24. Put a box around the words: **"One day he asked the woman. . ."** Draw a line from the box to the margin and write the words: "Eve listened to the lie." Like this:

Eve listened to the lie. — One day he asked the woman,

Of course, we will never listen to a snake talk! But that doesn't mean we don't listen to lies. Satan uses other things to lie to us—like friends, famous people, music, TV, or social media. Take Zoey, for example. She hung out with and listened to a friend who told her, "You **need** this app!"

Believing a lie always begins by simply listening to something that's not true. You don't have to touch it, do it, agree with it, or even like it. You just have to be close enough to **listen** to it. **(Don't do that!)**

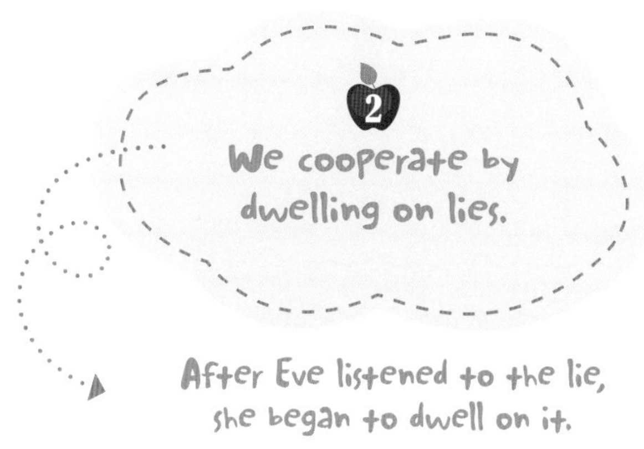

After Eve listened to the lie, she began to dwell on it.

Grab your ORANGE pencil and put a box around the words: "You must not eat it or even touch it; if you do, you will die." Next, draw a line from the box to the margin and write: "Eve dwelled on the lie."

Remember, dwelling is kind of like thinking about something **all the time**, **EVERY DAY**. This is what Eve did. And, she ended up changing what God said. **He didn't say they couldn't touch the fruit**. Eve added that. When we start to listen to lies, we sometimes make God's rules harder than they are, or we change them just a little. **And**, most importantly, we forget they exist to protect us.

Zoey began to dwell on the rules her parents created to protect her. She got obsessed thinking about the **one** way she couldn't connect with her friends instead of thinking about all the ways she **could**. She felt lonely and disconnected.

When we think too much about things we want but can't have, our feelings sometimes stick to us like glue rather than coming and going like they're supposed to do. Maybe we think about a movie we should not watch or an expensive pair of jeans. Or maybe it's even a good thing, like getting an A, but we think about it too much. It's easy to think about all the things that we don't have, but it's not okay when we do this **all the time**, **EVERY DAY**.

3

We cooperate by believing lies rather than the Truth of God's Word.

By listening to and dwelling on Satan's lies, Eve began to BELIEVE the lie rather than the Truth of what God had said.

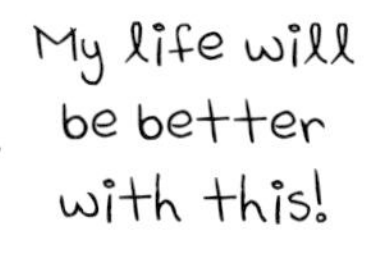

Go to page 25, and draw a PURPLE box around the words underlined in purple. Next, draw a line from the box to the margin and write:

"Eve believed the lie."

A lie that Eve believed:

"My life will be better with that fruit!"

It wasn't true at all. Her life was not better! Instead, the fruit took her life away. Eve didn't die **physically** on the day she first sinned, but she did die **spiritually**. And her body immediately began to slowly age, and would eventually die. On top of that, she and Adam felt embarrassed right away, and tried to hide from God by sewing big fig leaves together to cover their naked bodies.

Just like Eve, we all have to choose God's Truth or Satan's lies. There's no in-between. And, in almost every situation, we believe this lie:

"My life will be better with

______________________________!"

Fill in the blank with something that sometimes tempts you.

We all know what Zoey would write: **the app**! Zoey believed the lie that her life would be better with it. But it isn't true, as you'll soon see.

Grab your GREEN pencil and look at Genesis 3:1–7 on page 25 one last time. Draw a box around the words underlined in green, then draw a line to the margins. Write: "Eve acted on the lie."

Every sin begins with believing a lie.

That's exactly what happened to Zoey. She became a girl who craved social media. And then, she sinned. She disobeyed her mom and dad when she downloaded that app.

Let's see how she's doing.

Zoey isn't enjoying life as much as she thought she would. She feels guilty. Plus, she's always hiding from her mom! She feels afraid of being caught **all the time**, **EVERY DAY**. Zoey is learning that sin has consequences.

The moment we believe and act on a lie, we begin to experience the bad results of our actions. We have more bad thoughts and feelings. Satan's ultimate goal is our destruction and death, but until then, he just likes to make us feel **miserable**.

If you aren't careful, you could end up like Zoey. Even though she is our made-up friend, **her story is not fiction**. It's a real story that a 10-year-old girl and her mom told me. It caused a lot of tears and complications in their relationship.

Oh, you might not struggle with downloading an app and hiding it from your parents, but maybe there is something else you want so bad that you are in danger of acting on a lie.

CONSEQUENCE

"the result of a particular action or situation"

You might eventually . . .

steal something you can't afford.

You might eventually . . .

cheat on a test so you can get an A.

You might eventually . . .

lie to a friend about something you've done.

You might eventually . . .

say mean things to your sibling.

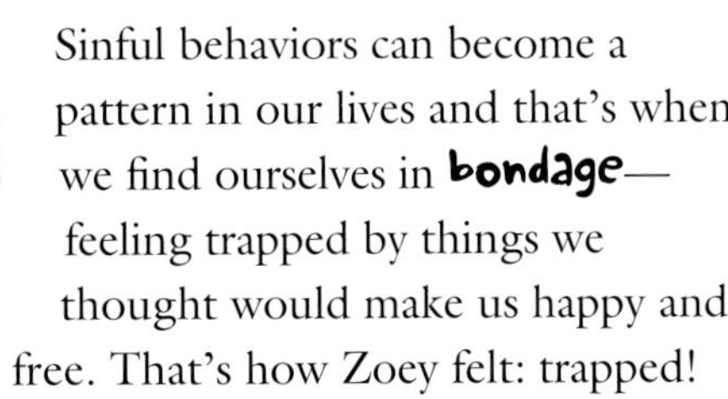

Sinful behaviors can become a pattern in our lives and that's when we find ourselves in **bondage**—feeling trapped by things we thought would make us happy and free. That's how Zoey felt: trapped!

This story has a cool ending that I will share soon. But first: let's figure out what to do when you feel all wrapped up in "sticky" feelings and realize that you're struggling with lies.

BONDAGE

"the state of being tied up or controlled by . . . something"[4]

Jesus Is Truth

(Who can set you free?)

I'm the worst person on the planet, and I feel sooo alone. My parents took my tablet away. I probably won't be allowed on social media until I'm like **20**! I'm freakin' out! I'm pretty sure my parents will never trust me again. I feel so distant from my mom. And I'm so embarrassed that I don't want to go to school tomorrow. My friends are going to ask, **"Why aren't you online?"** Tomorrow is going to be the worst day ever.

Like Zoey, have you ever felt worse than other people because of your sin? Or maybe you didn't feel sad about your sin, but you were embarrassed by your punishment. You're not alone. I've been there, too.

I have tried a lot of things to make me feel better when I sin, or when I get caught—like hiding at home or avoiding people. But that doesn't fix the way I feel inside. The only thing that has ever truly helped me is God's Truth. So, let's get serious about understanding Truth.

THE DEFINITION OF TRUTH

Here is an important definition for truth:

TRUTH: "agreement with a standard or original"

You might be asking: "Well, okay, um . . . what's a 'standard or original?'" Determining a standard or original for some things is really easy. For example, if you and some friends look at the same field, no one says the color of the grass is purple. This is because we've all learned the standard or original for identifying colors: the color wheel. And we know that the color of most healthy and watered grass is green. People agree this is true, because we have a standard by which we identify color.

Easy peasy!

But what is the standard or original to help us figure out the Truth about ourselves and our behaviors? Your feelings might make you ask some of these questions:

Fear could make you wonder,

- "Is it true that getting my period will be awful?"

A disagreement with your mom or dad may have you ask,

- "Is it true that my parents just don't and never will 'get me'?"

Discomfort could make you wonder,

- "Is it true that it's weird to talk to my mom about boys?"

You need a standard or original to help you decide what is true about these and other hard questions that your feelings bring up. So, let me point the way!

JESUS CHRIST IS TRUTH

Jesus is the standard and original source of what is true about us and about how we should act. He said:

TRUTH NUGGET: "I am the way, the truth, and the life." (John 14:6)

He is the definition of Truth. If you ask Him, He will reveal the Truth to you. He does this mostly through the written Word of God—the Bible! In fact, "the Word" is actually one of Jesus' names (John 1:14).

In the Bible, you'll find words that describe **WHO YOU ARE and HOW YOU SHOULD ACT**!

Let's test it out on our friend, Zoey. She feels trapped by a lot of "sticky" feelings. After she disobeyed her parents, she started believing more lies about herself.

Let's help her. She will tell us what her "sticky" feelings are making her believe. Then, I'll give her some advice using Bible verses because they contain Truth. Next, I'll ask you to write down what you might say to her.

Hey, Zoey! It's gonna be okay. We're here for you!

ZOEY: I'm the worst person on the planet! I feel so alone.

DANNAH: Romans 3:23 tells us that all of us sin, Zoey. You're **NOT** alone, and it is not true that you are the worst person on the planet. You're just like everyone else. I wish you hadn't downloaded that app, but believing another lie is not going to make you feel better.

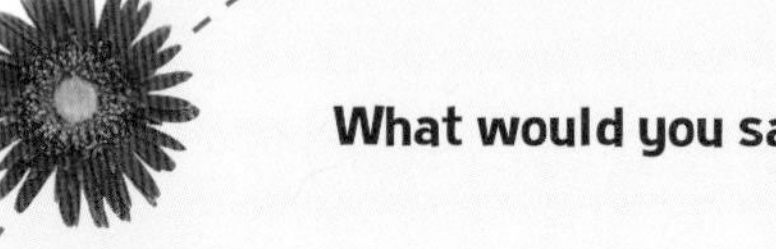

What would you say to Zoey?

ZOEY: I'm so embarrassed. Tomorrow is going to be the worst day ever.

DANNAH: Matthew 6:34 tells us to let God take care of tomorrow. Why don't you take time to pray and ask God to take care of the day? It is true that you have to face your friends and tell them you lost your tablet, but the best thing to do is to trust God with what will happen.

What would you say to Zoey?

Zoey, now that you've heard the Truth, how do you feel?

"I actually feel better. I guess it's true that everyone sins. And it feels sooooo good to let God take care of what my day will be like tomorrow!

Zoey has identified two of the lies she was believing, and replaced them with Truth. Instead of feeling trapped, she is beginning to feel free.

TRUTH SETS YOU FREE

Just as there are bad consequences to believing lies, there are also good results when we believe Truth.

TRUTH NUGGET:
"The truth will set you free." (John 8:32)

As Zoey hears the Truth, she feels better. It will take some time to get her tablet back and earn her parents' trust, but she already feels less trapped. That's how the Truth works.

Of course, it would have been better if Zoey had never believed the lies and acted on them at all. I want you to live in freedom and avoid feeling trapped by your feelings, lies, and sin. So, I've created a Truth Lab for you. Here, you'll practice identifying lies and replacing them with Truth. I can't wait to show you how.

Lies Girls Believe and the Truth That Sets Them Free

(Your Truth Lab)

There is **nooooo WAY** I want to live through that kind of thing again. Believing those lies led to the **biggest, baddest day** of my entire life. I never want to believe another lie in my life. I don't like how they make me feel.

Dannah

I don't like how lies make me feel either, Zoey. Remember, even so-called **BAD** feelings can be a good thing. They are signals from your heart warning you that something is wrong. God uses those feelings to communicate with us. It's when we don't know what to do with them, or when they just stick to us and never leave us, that something might be wrong. But sometimes it's really difficult to tell **WHAT**. I mean, the thing about a lie is that it can be tricky and confusing. So, I've created a **TRUTH LAB** for you and for other girls like you!

Sometimes when problems need to be solved, smart people spend time sorting through information in a laboratory, or lab. They're trying to find out what is true about something: the way our bodies heal, the secret to flying to the moon in a spaceship, or the way an animal responds to training. They are discovering and protecting truth for us, and for people who live in the future.

We need to discover and protect Truth to help us with our problems! There are so many lies confusing us that we need a place to organize and label the Truth. Otherwise, it might be lost forever. So, welcome to our Truth Lab!

This is where my team and I have organized important Truth for you. We have also uncovered **20 of the most common lies** girls like you believe and clearly **labeled them as lies**.

Building Our TRUTH LAB

It was not easy to figure out **20** of the most important Truths girls your age need. And it wasn't easy to find the most common lies girls believe. Here's how we did it.

First, I traveled to **11** cities to meet with mothers of girls your age. They helped me figure out the important Truth you need, and where the lies **might** be hiding.

But, we had to be sure!

Next, we asked girls just like you to answer some important questions. I was so happy to have **1,531** girls respond.

THE RESULT: We uncovered 20 of the common lies girls believe and identified the Truth they need to overcome them. Let's get into the Truth Lab to discover the Truth that can set you and other girls like you free.

TRUTH

Truth and Lies about God

CHAPTER 4

I'm glad that whole **thing** with the app is over. I do feel better since you helped me think about the Truth. But I have a question: is God mad at me? **I know He loves me . . .** it feels like He may be far away because of what I did. Does He love me **even** when I do something bad?

Zoey is in the right place for us to dig into the Bible for the Truth that sets all of us girls free. She wonders if God loves her even after she sins. Have you ever wondered that? Truth #1 is good news for all of us.

TRUTH #1 **God loves you *all the time*, no matter what!**

92% of girls are sure God loves them.

It's great that so many girls believe God loves them, but the Truth is even better. God loves 100% of humans **all the time**, no matter what. And that includes you!

God loves you. A lot!

The Bible tells us this Truth over and over. One of my favorite verses is Isaiah 43:4, which includes the simple words: "I love you."

Even so, I discovered that this Truth is hard for some girls to believe when they have done something bad, like disobey their parents or cheat on a test.

Sometimes their feelings tell them a lie about God's love. 

LIE: "GOD ONLY LOVES ME WHEN I'M GOOD."

Have you ever believed that lie? I think most of us have at some point in our lives. Sin makes it difficult to **feel** God's love even though it is still there. Trying to feel connected to God after we sin can be like trying to download a song or listen to an episode of *Adventures in Odyssey* when you don't have good Wi-Fi. The connection is there, but something is interfering with it.[6]

Sin makes it hard for us to connect clearly to God. (I'm going to explain more about that in another chapter.) **But God is still there. And He still loves you!** Yes, He feels sad when you sin and sometimes there are consequences, but that doesn't mean He doesn't love you. Let's see what our Truth Lab is storing up from God's Word.

TRUTH NUGGET: **"But God showed his great love for us by sending Christ to die for us while we were still sinners."** **(Romans 5:8)**

God is not surprised by your sin. He knows **EVERYTHING**. No matter what you have done or how much you have messed up, God still loves you and will forgive you.

I understood this better after I became a mother. Once when my son was little, he asked for water. He then promised he had **not** played with the lit candle in the other room. **That seemed like a funny thing to say!** (And, by that time, I could smell smoke.) Thankfully, only the edge of a blanket had caught on fire, and I was able to put it out quickly. You know what? Even as I rescued him from his own mistake, I did not love him any less. In fact, I put that fire out **because of love**. I wanted to keep him safe.

How much more does God, in all of His perfection, love you? He loves you when you behave well **and** when you behave badly.

I've asked Dannah to start by looking at the lies girls believe about God. Nothing is more important than this. If you believe things about God that are not true, you will end up believing lots of other things that are not true.

"There is nothing we can do to make God love us more. . . . there is nothing we can do to make God love us less."

—Philip Yancey[7]

God is all you need, because He loves you and will supply anything else you really need. Eve didn't believe this wonderful Truth. Instead, she believed: **My life would be better if I just had a bite of that fruit!**

Way back then, she faced a lie that some girls still believe.

TODAY GIRLS SAY THINGS LIKE:

- "My life would be better if I had STRAIGHT As!"
- "My life would be better if I had a PET!"
- "My life would be better if I had a FRIEND!"

Almost every girl has believed that last lie. When I talked to girls, they said things like, **"The most important part of church is good friends."** Or, **"The reason we picked my church is that I have friends there."** What they were saying is: **"God is not enough. I need a friend too."**

My friends help me grow closer to God, and to make good choices. I hope yours do, too. But our friends shouldn't be more important than God. Check out this Truth Lab Bible verse.

TRUTH NUGGET: "God who takes care of me will supply all your needs from his glorious riches . . ." (Philippians 4:19)

There is nothing wrong with having friends, a great family vacation, or a cute pair of jeans. Sometimes they **are** a great addition to our lives. But none of these things are as good or as useful as God. He is the one who gives us everything—our friendships, our brains, the pets we love, the money we use to buy clothes, and more. Only He can ever be enough.

My real live friend, 10-year-old Jenna Jones, has grown up in Germany where her parents are missionaries. Here's how she learned that Truth.

Jenna Jones, Berlin, Germany

"For the very first time ever I was going to live in America for a year. I was so scared. I thought to myself, 'I don't want to go. I won't have any friends.'"

Her family arrived in the United States during summer break, and Jenna **decided** to try to be happy even without friends. As weeks went by, she experienced a better friendship with Jesus. She had no idea what a good friend He could be. She began to believe she could do anything, if God was with her. That included going to a new school with no friends.

Then came the first day of school. The morning was hard, as friends greeted each other and caught up. All morning, she tried to concentrate on her schoolwork and kept quietly asking God for help. She couldn't believe it, but she felt okay.

Little did she know, God had a gift waiting.

"At recess, I made a lot of friends when we played soccer together."

She believes God gave her those friends. Sometimes He is capable of making friends in ways that we could never dream.

God wants to be the most important person in your life. And—pay close attention to this—He wants you to know that you can be content and even happy if He chooses not to give you something you want. Jenna was content through her summer and that first morning at school even though she didn't have any friends yet. He wants you to know the Truth that He alone is **enough**.

GOD + YOU = ENOUGH!

TRUTH #3 You are a Christian if you believe in Jesus and receive Him as your Savior.

When I looked at the answers 1,531 girls gave me for my questions about Truth and lies, I saw something sad.

22% percent of girls who claim to be a Christian do not understand how to become one.

THESE GIRLS SAID THINGS LIKE:

- I am a Christian because I go to church.
- I am a Christian because my mom and dad are Christians.
- I am a Christian because I have always been one.

Uh-oh! We have a big problem. There is a lie lurking, and it's hiding behind a lot of different things.

LIE: "I AM A CHRISTIAN BECAUSE ____________."

Going to church can be great, but it does not make you a Christian. Having parents who are Christians is awesome, but that does not make you a Christian either. And, no one has "always been one."

HOW DO YOU BECOME A CHRISTIAN?

I'm glad you asked. God loves us so much He sent His Son Jesus to die on the cross for us. The Bible says it this way:

TRUTH NUGGET: **"For this is how God loved the world: He gave his one and only Son, so that everyone who believes in him will not perish but have eternal life."** (John 3:16)

Why did Jesus die for us? He died because of our sin.

We have already talked about sin, but let's review. When we disobey God or choose to do wrong, we sin. Things like being mean, lying, or cheating are examples of sin. The Bible says that every single human who ever walked the earth has sinned. That includes you and me.

Sin separates us from God. And the Bible says the punishment for sin is death. **BUT GOD LOVES US**, so He sent His Son Jesus to die on a cross. The great news is that Jesus didn't stay dead. He came back to life with the power to forgive our sins. And, He offers us the free gift of His salvation.

I don't know about you, but I've never gotten a free gift without having to reach out to accept it. You accept God's free gift of salvation by **believing** in Jesus and **receiving** Him as your Savior.

TO **BELIEVE** IN JESUS MEANS:

- to trust Jesus
- to know Jesus is God's Son
- to know Jesus saves you from your sin
- to be willing to give Jesus control of your life

DO YOU BELIEVE IN JESUS?

If so, you are ready to **receive** Jesus as your Savior, which means you ask Jesus to live inside of you and be in charge of your life. Romans 10:9 reads, "If you openly declare that Jesus is Lord and believe in your heart that God raised him from the dead, you will be saved."

Have you ever received Jesus by asking Him to forgive you of your sins? If not, would you pray this prayer now?

Dear Lord, I admit to you that I am a sinner. I thank you for sending Jesus to die on the cross for my sins. I ask you to forgive me of my sins. I invite you to come into my life to be my Lord. Thank you for saving me. In Jesus' Name, Amen.

**Did you just pray that prayer for the first time?
If so, write the date below.**

The date I became a Christian:

Congratulations! Now, be sure to tell someone like your mom or your pastor. They're going to be so excited!

I hope the person you tell is also a Christian and can help you grow. Remember, you've just given Jesus control of your life. This mean's you'll obey Him and do what He asks you to do. Praying that prayer is just the first step in being a Christian. Now, your life needs to be lived as if you have changed. Ask this person to help you know how to grow.

At the end of each chapter, I'll remind you of the topics we examined in the Truth Lab. Then, you get to help Zoey by giving her some advice. Finally, you get to answer some questions that help **you** tell yourself Truth.

PUT ON YOUR LAB COAT

THE LIE	THE TRUTH
God only loves me when I am good.	• **God loves you all the time, every day.** (Isaiah 43:4) • **God loves you even though you sin.** (Romans 5:8)
God is not enough.	• **God is all you need.** (Psalm 23:1) • **God provides all your needs.** (Philippians 4:19) • **Jesus wants to be your best friend.** (John 15:15)
I am a Christian because ________________.	• **You become a Christian when you believe Jesus is the Son of God who died for your sins . . .** (John 3:16) • **. . . and you ask Him to live inside you and be in charge of your life.** (Romans 10:9)

TELLING MYSELF THE TRUTH

It's your turn to be the author!

- Have you believed any of these lies about God? Put an X on top of any of **THE LIES** in this chapter that you have believed.
- What Truth do you need to think about **all the time**, **EVERY DAY**? Look at **THE TRUTH** we dug up together. Now circle what seems important for you personally to dwell on.
- Next, begin to think about it **all the time**, **EVERY DAY**. You can start by writing a prayer to God, a helpful Bible verse, or some ideas you don't want to forget in the space below.

Helping Zoey Believe Truth

It's time to give Zoey some advice!

Zoey feels far away from God because she lied to her parents. Based on what you learned in this chapter, is God really as far away as Zoey feels He is? What can she do to feel closer to her parents?

Lies about Myself

A new girl moved into our neighborhood this week. Her name is Isabella and her long legs make her run fast. So, of course, she got picked first for kickball today. Who got picked *last?* ME! The girl with the **SHORT** legs. **Again!!!**

Zoey isn't alone! When it comes to kickball, I remember being picked last too—over and over again. It felt really bad. But when I discovered the Truth, it helped a lot. I believe it'll help you too.

TRUTH #4 God chose you!

You are the work of THE Master Artist, God. The Bible says that He **knit** you together, which means He carefully planned and crafted you.

Have **you** ever done any knitting? It requires **MATH**! It's careful and precise. If you don't count correctly, your knitting will turn into a mess. The stitches have to be accurate, or the appearance will be super sloppy!

Here's the point: God didn't just randomly throw a bunch of stuff together and say, "Uh oh! Will you look at that? I guess I made an Emma!" (Or a Zaani or a Chloe.) Nope! He carefully planned and made you. Every ability you have was planned by God.

Even so, there might be days when you don't feel so good about yourself. It happens.

SOMETIMES, GIRLS HAVE THOUGHTS LIKE THESE:

- I'm not smart enough.
- I'm not strong enough.
- I'm not fast enough.
- I'm not funny enough.
- Or, fill in the blank: I'm not ______________________ enough.

These thoughts happen when we compare ourselves to other people, and listen to the opinions of others. One way we see the opinion of others is when they choose us . . . or when they don't.

It **hurts** not to be chosen. I remember how I felt when it happened to me: rejected, embarrassed, and judged.

My thoughts about it grew into a big, fat lie.

LIE: "I'M NOT GOOD ENOUGH."

This lie comes with some serious "sticky" feeling super glue. When we start to believe this lie, it's about more than our kickball skills or our math grade. It feels like we wear an all-out-nasty label that defines us.

Guess what!? Jesus understands. He also had people judging Him, overlooking Him, rejecting Him, and "not choosing" Him! The Bible says Jesus understood the weaknesses humans face, and He even had the same temptations as you and me. Since we are tempted to believe we are not good enough, it is likely that He was too. Though we don't know exactly how, Isaiah 53:2 tells us that He wasn't especially good-looking. He had at least this **one** thing about Him that was "less than" others around Him.

I'm pretty sure He was aware of this, **BUT** . . . the Bible tells us He never sinned. That means He never believed any lies! So, why didn't Jesus ever believe the lie that He wasn't good enough?

Well, 1 Peter 2:4 tells us that "Christ . . . was rejected by people, but he was chosen by God for great honor." **JESUS** was rejected by men. People said things about Him that were not good, **but He didn't listen to those opinions. Instead, He chose to believe what God the Father said about Him**. That was the only opinion that mattered to Him, and the one He used to decide what to believe about Himself.

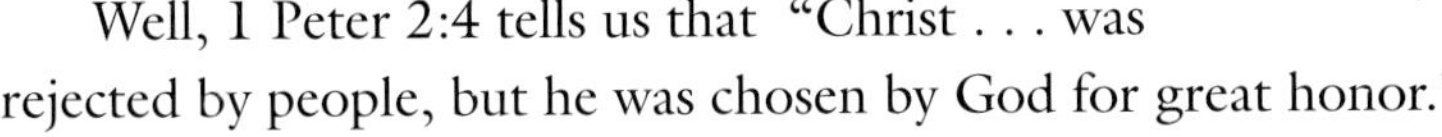

Let's look at what God says about YOU to help you know what to believe about yourself.

TRUTH NUGGET: "Even before he made the world, God loved us and chose us in Christ to be holy and without fault in his eyes." (Ephesians 1:4)

Your confidence is always going to nose-dive if you compare yourself to others, and listen to their opinion of you. Stop obsessing about who did not choose you! Instead, **focus on the One who has chosen you!**

START LISTENING TO AND BELIEVING GOD'S OPINION ABOUT YOU.

He knows the Truth.

And the Truth is, God chose you, and He'd choose you every time.

TRUTH #5 The beauty that matters most to God is on the inside of me.

Do you love the way you look? If your immediate answer is no, you're not alone. The lie I'm about to reveal is kind of related to the last one. A lot of girls say, **"I'm not pretty enough!"** But the beauty problem is so big, it deserves its very own Truth statement.

Almost half of the girls we talked to are not happy with how they look.[8] When we asked them what part of their face or body they didn't like, the number one answer was their weight. Sometimes they thought they weighed too much, and sometimes too little.

THEY WROTE THINGS LIKE:

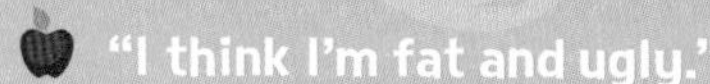

- "I think I'm fat and ugly."
- "I like my freckles, but I wish I were taller and weighed more."

I know this is partly because we are surrounded by pretty girls on TV, on YouTube, in movies, and in ads. And, because these girls get a lot of attention and sometimes become famous, it's easy to compare ourselves to them.

It's also easy to believe a big lie.

LIE: "PRETTY GIRLS ARE WORTH MORE."

Let's ask an important question to fight this lie: **Are these "pretty girls" really as perfect as they look?** The Bible warns that beauty can **sometimes** fool you and that it **always** fades. There are often so many special effects applied to photos of "pretty" girls that if you met them in real life you might not recognize them. This is what one of them said about a photo that was supposed to show her with no makeup.

Sadie Robertson, Louisiana, United States

"... the director of the shoot took a quick look at me and said, 'Nope this girl does not have the face to pull off... no makeup!' They proceeded to spend around two hours making it look as though I had no makeup on. Let's be real I did NOT wake up like that."[9]

It took two hours to put on Sadie's makeup for her "no makeup" photo!

The Bible tells us things like hairstyles, nice clothes, and jewelry are not what God considers beautiful. The physical qualities that are so important to us are not worth much to God.

Let's find Truth in the Bible to replace that lie.

TRUTH NUGGET:

"The Lord doesn't see things the way you see them. People judge by outward appearance, but the Lord looks at the heart." (1 Samuel 16:7)

I so want you to concentrate on the beauty that matters most: your heart. You become most beautiful to God when you get excited about wearing things like kindness, helpfulness, and cheerfulness, rather than some cool new shoes, or a great lip gloss.

Nowhere does the Bible say it's bad to want to be beautiful or to appreciate beauty in someone else. But it is wrong to go crazy over physical beauty without being concerned with the beauty of our hearts. So spend time learning how to be helpful. Ask someone to help you be more truthful. Or practice giving by saving some money and giving it to your church or to someone who has a special need. These are the things God finds beautiful!

TRUTH #6 You're ready for more responsibility.

Did you know that "teenagers" and "tweens" are actually modern inventions? A long time ago those words didn't exist. You know what did? Responsibility!

Way back when Jesus was alive, a 12-year-old **wanted** to earn responsibility. He or she was expected to be wise, mature, and responsible.

A girl might walk a long distance to fetch water for her family each morning, or make bread for the family dinner each evening. She knew that not doing those things would result in a thirsty or hungry family. Back then, girls who were 8 or 9 were thinking about learning to **DO** things.

RESPONSIBILITY

"doing things that you are expected to do and accepting the results of your actions"[10]

It took nearly 2,000 years for that to change. Kids became less interested in responsibility when they were distracted by new things like cars, movie theaters, and makeup. As people started to make these things, they also invented the words "teen" and "tween"[11] so they could convince those age groups that they needed to buy stuff. They told girls that they needed **things**. The result? Today, a lot of girls want to **HAVE** things.

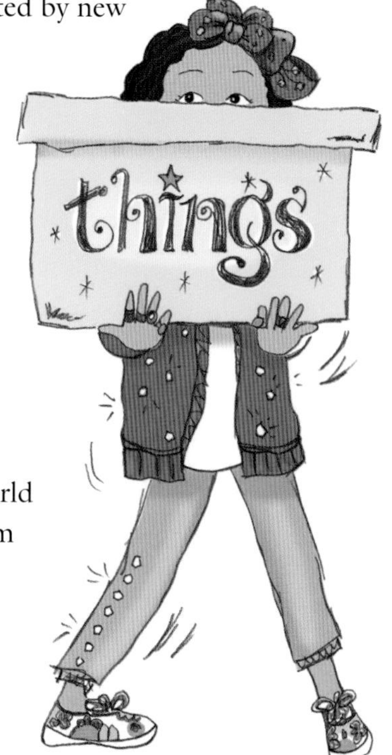

And sometimes they are things adults—parents, teachers, or lawmakers—think girls are not ready to have yet. **Some** girls think their world has too many rules if they can't have the freedom to have anything they want.

And when they think about that a whole lot, they begin to believe a lie.

37% OF GIRLS SAY THEY NEED MORE FREEDOM.

If you are one of them, I have a question to ask: What do you want to do with your freedom? Circle one.

I want freedom to HAVE things like makeup or a phone and to go to parties.

OR

I want freedom so I can DO things for others and be trusted with more responsibilities.

I hope you circled the second one, but I'm thankful for your honesty if you circled the first one. Based on my conversations with tween girls, a lot of them would most likely circle the first one because they grumbled really loud when they said things like:

"I HAVE to do chores!"

"My parents make me do a ridiculous amount of jobs, but they don't let me have anything good like a cellphone or makeup!"

It sounded to me like some of them were complaining about having responsibilities. Time to put grumbling attitudes into the Truth Lab.

TRUTH NUGGET:
"Do everything without complaining and arguing." (Philippians 2:14)

The time will come when you are in charge of decisions, but you must prove your readiness. Look for chances to practice responsibility, not freedom.

Instead of complaining, "I **HAVE** to do chores," a mature girl says, "I **GET** to do chores." It is a good thing to be helpful to those you love and live with. Being a tween means that it's time for you to begin to grow up. Even Jesus had to **GROW** in wisdom and maturity (Luke 2:52). He didn't just have His freedom given to Him because He was the Son of God!

PUT ON YOUR LAB COAT

Grab your pencils. It's your turn to work in our Truth Lab.

THE LIE	THE TRUTH
I'm not good enough.	• **God chose you.** (Ephesians 1:7) • **We are not "good enough" without God, but He is our "enough."** (2 Corinthians 3:5) • **You are wonderfully made.** (Psalm 139:13–14; Ephesians 2:10)
Beautiful girls are worth more.	• **God looks at my heart.** (1 Samuel 16:7)
I need more freedom.	• **You're ready for more responsibility.** (Luke 2:52) • **God wants you to embrace responsibility without grumbling or complaining.** (Philippians 2:14)

TELLING MYSELF THE TRUTH

It's your turn to be the author!

- Have you believed any lies about yourself? Put an X on top of any of **THE LIES** in this chapter that you have believed.
- What Truth do you need to think about **all the time**, **EVERY DAY**? Look at **THE TRUTH** we dug up together, and circle what seems important to dwell on.
- Next, begin to think about it **all the time**, **EVERY DAY**. You can start by writing a prayer to God, a helpful Bible verse, or some ideas you don't want to forget in the space below.

Helping Zoey Believe Truth

It's time to give Zoey some advice!

Zoey got picked last and felt really bad about it. In fact, she started to believe some lies, because she said she "deserved" it. If you could encourage her, how would you help her believe Truth?

Lies about Family

Argh! My little brother and I got into a fight. **AGAIN!** We're always arguing. My friend told me **EVERYONE** in the world fights with their little brothers, and it's no big deal. If that's true, why do I feel so bad about it? **This is the same friend that told me to lie to my parents about downloading that app!!! I don't think it's really okay to fight with my brother.**

Just like Zoey, maybe you fight with your siblings, or maybe even your parents. Sometimes a family can feel like a gift you wish you could take back. But there's no return department that accepts parents or siblings! So, we have to sort through the lies about our families. Here's an important Truth to believe about your family.

Think back to the last lie, "I need more freedom." One of the reasons girls feel the need for freedom is because of the rules in their family. Sometimes these rules are different from the rules their friends' families have.

This makes some girls believe a lie.

LIE: "MY FAMILY IS SOOOO WEIRD."

But rules were not the **only** reason they believed this lie. I counted **171 reasons** why girls believed they had a super crazy family.

HERE ARE JUST A FEW OF THE THINGS GIRLS SAID:

- "We do not eat sugar."
- "It's a foster family and we have a lot of kids."
- "I'm adopted."
- "We are different colors."
- "We're a pastor's family, and it's abnormal."
- "We live in India."
- "We raise GOATS! GOATS!"
- "We are HUGE! There are seven people in this HOUSE!!!"
- "We live on a farm, and we are homeschooled."
- "My parents are artists, so we are all a bit weird."
- "I'm so different. My family is so indescribable."

A lot of these girls said their lives would be better if their families were "**just** a little" more like everyone else's. They **want** to be normal, but is that what's best? For example, many of them reported fighting with their siblings . . . a lot!

81% of girls fight with their siblings.

When we asked how they felt about it, there were two opinions that were most common.

47% said, "I wish we didn't."

34% said, "It's okay. It's normal!"

Some girls may think it's normal to fight with your siblings, BUT that doesn't mean it's okay. The Bible instructs us to "do all" we can "to live in peace with everyone." That includes our brothers and sisters. When we fight without doing all we can to avoid it just because it's "normal," we are not living the way God created us to live. Being normal is not **best**.

NORMAL IS OVERRATED.

But you may still say, "But I can't eat sugar! What's the sin in **that**?" Or "My family has GOATS! Does it have to be that way?" Or "My family is too big. Why does my mom keep having babies?" Those things can make you feel weird, too. So, we still haven't solved your problem, have we?

Oh, look! I see we have dug ourselves straight down to a truth nugget. And just in time.

TRUTH NUGGET: "Don't copy the behavior and customs of this world, but let God transform you into a new person by changing the way you think. Then you will learn to know God's will for you, which is good and pleasing and perfect." (Romans 12:2)

The Bible tells us we are NOT supposed to be like everyone else. Instead, we should let God be in charge of how we think. The difference that should be seen in a Christian family is summed up well by a girl who wrote:

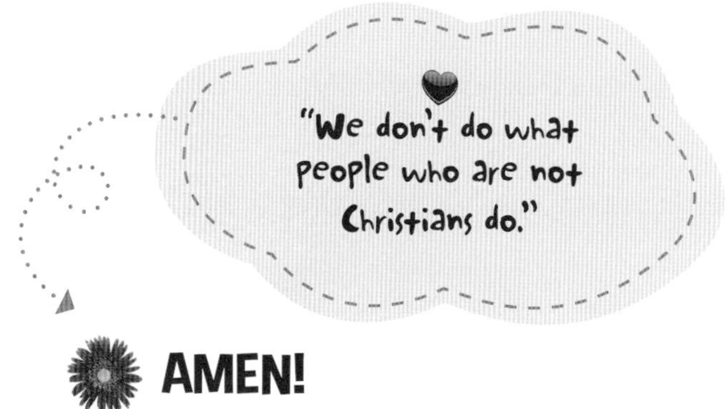

AMEN!

You might say, "But what does this have to do with not eating sugar?" Or maybe you want to know: "How does this Truth help me if I have the **HUGEST** family in church, and feel like we're kind of a freak show?"

Well, there are **SOME** things your parents do because God leads them to decisions that are unique. And when you really think about it, some of the things that make your life a little different are super cool. God asks some parents to adopt and some to be foster parents. He asks some to be missionaries in India and others to lead a church in Ohio.

And there are also **SOME** things your parents do just because they like it or believe it is best for your family, and it helps them practice being different. They might eat differently or be artistic or raise goats.

Your family is different. That's a good thing!

Of course, sometimes the differences in your family are truly painful. Let's talk about that next.

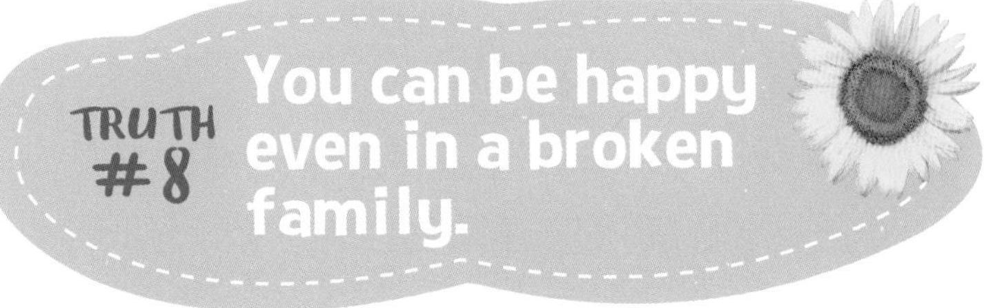

Some girls thought their family was weird because of divorce, overworking, sickness, and even death. In extreme cases, girls even questioned whether or not their parents loved them. A lot of our families are very broken.

- "My dad is in the hospital a lot. My mom is always angry, but I have my dog so that helps."
- "Dad is in jail."
- "I have a sick sister, so we're late for almost everything."
- "My dad is never home because he works third shift, and when he is home he just sleeps and gets angry."
- "My dad left us."
- "My parents are divorced."

I understand your pain. I have had some sad things happen in my own family that caused a lot of tears. It's okay to be sad when your family feels broken. God sees your pain. The Bible says He "keeps track of all [our] sorrows," and He has "recorded each one in [His] book" (Psalm 56:8). He would only do that if He cared and wanted to help you.

At the same time, He doesn't want us to **give in** to being constantly sad. It can be tempting to dwell on the sadness. That is, to think about it **all the time**, **EVERY DAY**, and maybe even believe it will never change.

Here's the problem with that: you might begin to believe a lie.

LIE: "MY FAMILY IS TOO BROKEN FOR ME TO EVER BE HAPPY."

When you believe the lie that you cannot be happy unless everything in your family and life are okay, you put your trust in the wrong places. Jesus wants you to hope in **HIM**, not in your family. The Truth is that happiness is not found in family, or in any human relationship. True joy can only be found in Jesus.

Let's dig deep to discover God's Truth.

TRUTH NUGGET: "I have learned how to be content with whatever I have." (Philippians 4:11)

Let me explain the word **content**. It's a little different from the kind of happiness you feel on Christmas morning. It's not the kind of happy you feel when all your friends come to your birthday party. It's a different kind of happy. It's quiet and peaceful. It's kind of like feeling okay.

The man who wrote the book of Philippians in the Bible understood that we may not be able to control the things that happen to us, but the things that happen don't have to control us. He went through some hard things, like being put in jail for talking about Jesus. Even there, he was content.

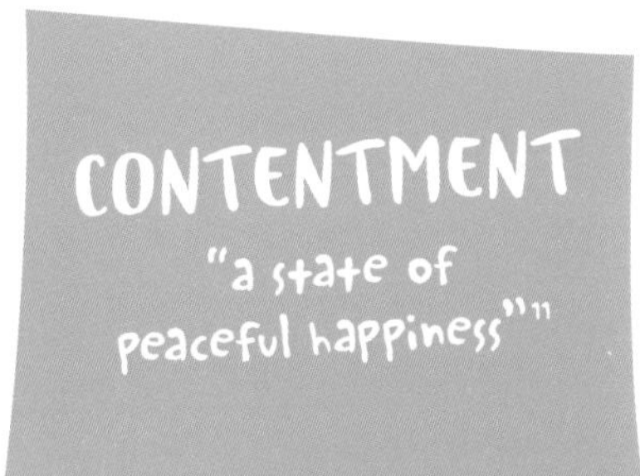

The Truth is that if you are not content with your family now, you may not be content your whole life because our world is broken, and bad things do happen.*

Nine-year-old Talia knows what it feels like to have a broken family. She was born to a mom who didn't have much money. They shared a bed, and Talia kept all her clothes in a garbage bag.

*There are some important exceptions to being content. If someone is hurting you, touching you in ways that make you feel uncomfortable, or saying a lot of cruel things to you, TELL SOMEONE! That is called abuse, and you should never be content with it.

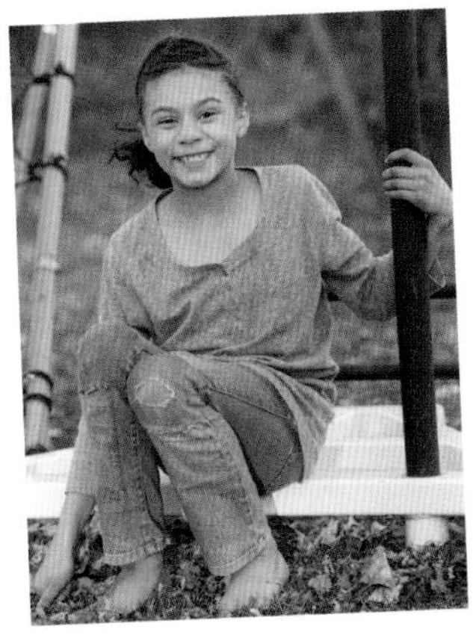

Talia Saum, Minnesota, United States

"I would often wake up, there was barely anything to eat. Sometimes my mom wasn't even at home, and I would just go back to sleep until she came home."

Things went from bad to worse when Talia had to go live in a home for children because her mom could not take care of her. Soon she went to live with a foster family. There, she heard about Jesus.

> *"I love that Jesus loves everyone no matter what they have done. He changed my life so much."*

Talia was adopted by her foster family when she was 7 years old, but there is always a part of her that is aware of how broken families can be.

> *"I pray for my birth parents to become Christians every night. And because of all I have been through, I like to do things for others now. I don't just want to think of myself, and what I need. I know what it's like to be hurt, and I know who I can trust—God."*

Talia has learned what it means to be content. Her story inspires me so much.

My mom was one of my best friends when I was growing up. A relationship like that is something to cherish, because not every girl shares a special friendship with her mom. If you're a girl who wishes she had this, you should know that even those of us who are friends with our moms have experienced the pain of feeling misunderstood.

For example, you might have a perfect day where you laugh a lot and eat cookie dough 'til you can't move. Just when you feel like your mom is the coolest thing on the planet, **things go bad!** You ask your best-friend-of-a-mom to go to a movie that "everyone else is seeing." But she says no. And then, she says, "I'm not raising one of the bunch. I'm raising a top banana!"

That's a real thing my mom said to me over and over again when I wanted to do something "everyone else was

doing." I admit that I often dramatically stomped off. Sometimes I gave my mom the silent treatment. **That wasn't cool!** **Why did I act that way?**

Well, sometimes I believed this lie.

LIE: "MY PARENTS JUST DON'T GET ME."

I sometimes felt like my parents were so old that they just couldn't understand me! Have you ever felt that way? This lie might show up with some other lies, such as: "I don't have to honor my parents because they're so old-fashioned," or "My mom (or dad) doesn't love me," or "My mom is **supposed** to be my best friend!" No matter what form it takes, you are at risk of believing this lie when you don't like the way your parents are . . . well, **parenting**.

What comes next is often ugly. (Did I mention stomping off, the silent treatment, arguing, throwing a fit, and being plain **RUDE** to my awesome mom?) We humans don't naturally obey, respect, and honor, do we? (Things just got real!)

I have a truth nugget for you. It's not very fancy because we just need straight-up truth.

TRUTH NUGGET:

"Children, obey your parents because you belong to the Lord, for this is the right thing to do. 'Honor your father and mother.' This is the first commandment with a promise: If you honor your father and mother, 'things will go well for you, and you will have a long life on earth.'" (Ephesians 6:1–3)

This verse doesn't need a lot of explaining. You are supposed to honor your parents, which means to treat them with respect.

5 PRACTICAL WAYS TO HONOR YOUR PARENTS

Accept their decisions, even if you don't love the decisions they make.

(Don't stomp off, argue, or give them the silent treatment.)

Ask for their advice because they are wise.

(I know you naturally want to ask your BFF about boys, friends, or God. But your mom and dad know a lot more on those topics.)

Speak well of them in front of others.

(You don't get to stop honoring them when they aren't around.)

Be respectful when you disagree.

(It's okay to tell your mom or dad that you don't like a decision they make, or that your opinion is different. Just do it nicely, and obey their decision even if you can't win them over.)

Forgive them when they sometimes get it wrong.

(They're imperfect and sinful, just like you. So be quick to forgive them. They've probably forgiven you a time or two!)

Here's the really great thing that happens when you start to practice this hard task of honoring your father and mother: **it feels good!**

It's called joy. It's the good feeling you get inside when things outside don't go your way. It comes from doing the right thing. This makes sense because our Truth Nugget tells us "things will go well for you" when you honor your parents.

Let me tell you an important fact:

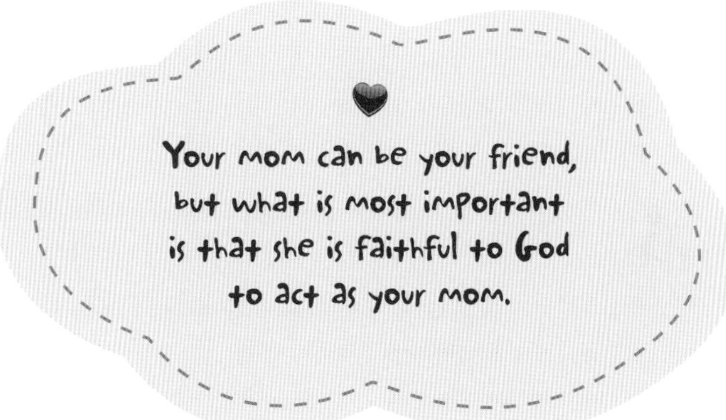

Above all, she is your parent. Let's not forget your dad. I know lots of girls with special father/daughter relationships. That should be treasured, but you should still remain faithful to honoring, respecting, and treating them both like parents.

PUT ON YOUR LAB COAT

Grab your pencils.
It's your turn to work in our Truth Lab.

THE LIE	THE TRUTH
My family is weird.	• **Your family is different. That is good.** (Romans 12:2) • **Normal is overrated.** (Ephesians 4:17,19–20) • **You should stick out.** (Philippians 2:15)
My family is too broken to be happy.	• **You can be happy even in a broken family.** (Philippians 4:12–13) • **God wants you to trust in Him, not your family.** (Psalm 118:8) • **You can learn to be content no matter what.** (Philippians 4:11,13)
My parents just don't get me.	• **Both your parents are to be honored.** (Ephesians 6:1–2) • **Obey your parents.** (Ephesians 6:1–2) • **God gives you joy when you honor your parents.** (Ephesians 6:3)

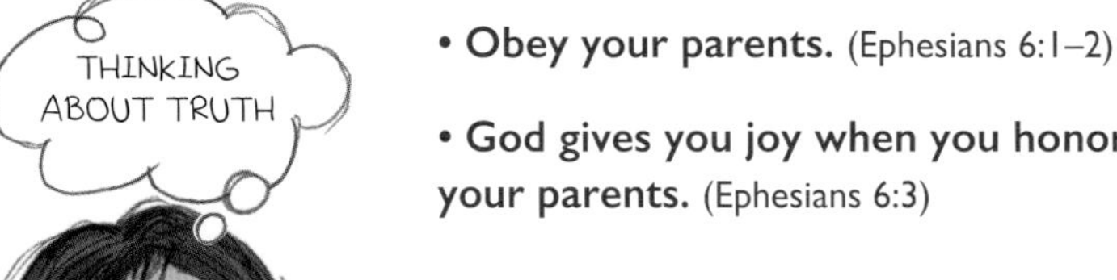

TELLING MYSELF THE TRUTH

It's your turn to be the author!

- Have you believed any of these lies about your family? Put an X on top of any of **THE LIES** in this chapter that you have believed.
- What Truth do you need to think about **all the time**, **EVERY DAY**? Look at **THE TRUTH** we dug up together. Now circle what seems important for you personally to dwell on.
- Next, begin to think about it **all the time**, **EVERY DAY**. You can start by writing a prayer to God, a helpful Bible verse, or some ideas you don't want to forget in the space below.

Helping Zoey Believe Truth

It's time to give Zoey some advice!

Zoey's friend told her that it's normal to fight with siblings.
Do you agree or disagree? Why or why not?
What do you think Zoey should do about fighting with her brother?

Lies about Sin

Gigi's my best friend. We tell each other **EVERYTHING**! Sometimes we just hang out for hours. But . . . not anymore. She **LIED** to me! Gigi said she was the **only** one invited to Emma's for a sleepover, but it turns out everyone in my class except ME was invited. When I called Gigi on it, she acted like it was **NO BIG DEAL**! She told me she lied so my feelings wouldn't be hurt!!!! She actually said that sometimes it's good to lie. I'm so mad! I feel like having a sleepover and not inviting her!

Zoey has discovered something important. Gigi's lie made her feel lonely. That's the thing about lies, they make us feel far away from others, including God. (And, by the way, even when we are trying to protect someone's feelings, lying is always a sin.) Let's dig into Truth #10!

TRUTH #10 Sin separates you from God.

I **know what it's like to feel the separation that sin creates.** When I was young, we weren't allowed to eat or drink in my dad's office. One super hot summer day, I needed to work in there, and I decided to take my drink with me. **BIG MISTAKE!** I spilled red juice all over the carpet. I cleaned and prayed, hoping my dad wouldn't notice.

But he did!

He asked me what happened. I just shrugged my shoulders as if to say, "I don't know."

It worked!!! My dad didn't punish me, or anything. I thought the whole thing was no big deal. **I had heard of worse sins than disobeying my dad or lying.**

Some girls, like me, think **their** sin is no big deal when people around them do things that seem worse. It's almost like we try to grade sin. Things like stealing or murder seem like **BIGGER, BADDER SINS**. Things like that get a big, ugly F. But does that mean things like lying or cheating or grumbling or being mean only get a B-?

Maybe you have believed the lie that I did.

LIE: "MY SIN ISN'T THAT BIG OF A DEAL."

If you have, you are not alone.

23% of girls believe that the sins of others were bigger and badder than their own.

THESE GIRLS SAID THINGS LIKE:

- I lie about cleaning my whole room or about brushing my teeth. It's really dumb.
- I blame stuff on my brother that I actually did.
- I have a habit of talking back to my parents.

If only we could understand that every single sin is a big deal. Every time we sin, we choose our way instead of God's way.

Do you remember how Adam and Eve hid from God after they sinned? It's because they began to feel far away from Him.

After I sinned by lying to my dad, I started to feel far away from him **and** from God too. The fun friendship I shared when my dad and I trained our German Shepherd dogs was awkward, and even going to dog shows together felt lonely. And when it came to God, I could hardly pray.

No matter how small or big a sin may seem, the result is the same.

TRUTH NUGGET: **"But your sins have separated you from your God."** **(Isaiah 59:2a NIrV)**

Are there any sins in your life that you don't think are a big deal? **Write them in the space below.**

What you just wrote separates you from God. Every sin does. And that feels bad, doesn't it?

Eve could have easily believed that her sin was not that big of a deal. After all, she didn't divorce Adam; she didn't swear at God, or say He doesn't exist. All she did was take a bite of something God told her not to eat. What was the big deal? The big deal was that God said, "Don't," and Eve said, "I will."[13]

If you like being in a happy relationship with God and others, it's a good idea to do your best to avoid sinning. But, when you do sin—which we all do sometimes and is exactly why we need Jesus—here's another important Truth Nugget for you.

TRUTH NUGGET: "But if we confess our sins to him, he is faithful and just to forgive us our sins." (I John 1:9)

Be quick to confess your sin. God is always ready to forgive you and welcome you back into friendship with Him. And, He'll even help you restore your friendships with others.

Speaking of others, do you want to know if I told my dad about the red juice? I'll tell you in the next section.

TRUTH #11 Hiding sin sets you up for failure.

A few weeks after I spilled the red juice and lied to my dad about it, my parents dropped me off at summer camp. I was so sure a week of pool time, the snack bar, and campfires would ease the guilt. I was wrong!

One night at a campfire, our counselor talked about sin and confession. The whole cabin started confessing really big sins. One girl said she had a secret boyfriend. Another one told us she had stolen something. And some shared even worse things.

Our counselor prayed with each girl, and then simply said to them, "I think you should call your parents."

There was **NOOOOO WAY** I was gonna tell my secret. **What if she made me tell my dad?**

Here's the thing. As we sat there in that room, I started to feel guilty. It was heavier than it had ever been. (My mom later told me that this feeling is called "conviction.") All this time, I had hoped I could wait the guilt out. But it just doesn't work that way. Guilt grows. It doesn't go away. I was miserable!

Suddenly, I couldn't stand it anymore.

"I did it! I spilled the red juice," I cried out.

The entire cabin stared at me wide-eyed. Yet no one made me feel like my sin was worse than theirs, or like it wasn't big enough to share. They just prayed with me. And then . . . my counselor said **IT**. The thing I dreaded most: **"I think you should call your dad."**

A lie I believed was quickly dying.

WE ASKED 1,531 GIRLS IF THEY HAD ANY SECRETS ABOUT SIN.

More than half said they do have secrets about sin.

We asked them to explain what they meant.

- **Some said they had a secret about their own sin.**
- **Some said they keep doing the same sin over and over again, but never talk to an adult to get help.**
- **Some said they knew about someone else's sin and thought they should tell an adult, but felt afraid.**

Maybe you too have believed that you don't need to tell anyone about your sin, or someone else's sin. There are a lot of lies that grow along with this one. Things like:

"No one needs to know about my sin in order for me to stop."

"It's always right to keep a secret."

"If I tell __________, they might not like or love me anymore."

Some girls try to manage their sinful situation by hiding it. They want to overcome it, avoid disappointing their parents, or keep their friends from hating them. But here's the super sad reality: hiding your sin results in the exact opposite.

TRUTH NUGGET: "People who conceal their sins will not prosper, but if they confess and turn from them, they will receive mercy." (Proverbs 28:13)

It is natural to want to conceal, or hide, sin. Everyone does it. Since the beginning of time when Adam and Eve hid, people have been hiding their sin. But the Bible says you will not succeed if you **keep** hiding your sin.

Remember Gigi's lie about the slumber party? Just like Gigi's lie was meant to protect Zoey and didn't, hiding your sin isn't really protecting you. Rather, it's probably going to get you into trouble and make you feel lonely. Why? Because when you hide your sin, you can't get the help you need.

It is hard to learn from a poor decision or sin, until you admit that you did it and confess it. It is also hard to figure out how to stop sinning without some help. Everyone sins, but the Bible says only a fool keeps doing the same thing over and over again.

I'm going to tell you the thing you may not want to hear:

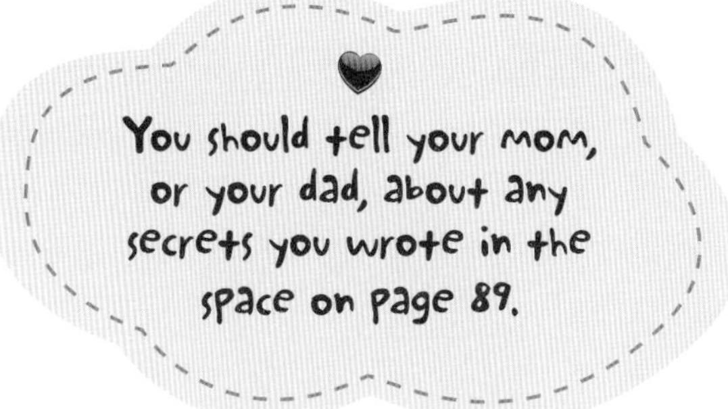

What you wrote in that box separates you from God if you have not confessed it to Him. And it might be getting in the way of your relationships with other people too. The Bible tells us to "confess your sins to each other" (James 5:16). Only God can forgive sins, but He wants us to confess to other people so we can get help.

It feels bad to hide your sin. You know what feels really great? Telling someone about your sin! It's one of the most freeing things I've ever done.

That night after the campfire, I called my dad. I told him what I had done, and asked for his forgiveness. He said, "Yeah, I know." The truth is he was way more disappointed that I was lying to him than he would have been if I had just confessed that I disobeyed him. And, he was really happy that I finally told him. He was just waiting for it, because he knew I would feel better. Telling my dad about my sin didn't make me feel worse. It made me feel better.

TRUTH #12 **Everything we see or hear should be true, noble, right, pure, lovely, worthy of respect, excellent, and praiseworthy.**

People spend a lot of money on entertainment. Movies. Music. The internet. Books. Apps. Because, well . . . they **entertain** us! But did you know that these things can also **change** us?

What we watch and listen to can change the way we think and how we behave, either in positive ways or negative ways depending on what we watch. Do you know why? Because it's kind of like "dwelling" on thoughts. (Remember that word from the beginning of the book?) When you think about something long enough, you could start believing it.

Be careful! You could give the control of your thoughts over to the entertainment world. It might be "normal" to watch and listen to anything you feel like, but remember: we must check our feelings with God's Truth. Let's do that now.

TRUTH NUGGET: "And now, dear brothers and sisters, one final thing. Fix your thoughts on what is true, and honorable, and right, and pure, and lovely, and admirable. Think about things that are excellent and worthy of praise." (Philippians 4:8)

This verse gives us some simple tests for all the movies, TV shows, songs, podcasts, books, and pictures or stories we see on the internet. Think about the last movie, TV show, or song you watched or listened to and **write the name of it here:**

____

NOW, LET'S RUN IT THROUGH THE TEST.

Check each box if the answer to the question is "yes."

☐ **Is it true?**
(There were *no* untruthful things in it, like teaching about evolution or saying that God is not real.)

☐ **Is it noble?**
(There were no scenes, lyrics, or situations that made bad things like drinking or drugs attractive.)

☐ **Is it right?**
(Your parents and teachers would say it was okay for you to see or listen to it.)

☐ **Is it pure?**
(People were dressed and speaking modestly.)

☐ **Is it lovely?**
(It did not leave you with ugly or violent thoughts or pictures.)

☐ **Is it worthy of respect?**
(You would show it to your parents, your pastor, your teachers, and others.)

☐ **Is it excellent?**
(It was created with care, and helped you use your imagination.)

☐ **Is it praiseworthy?**
(You would recommend it to others.)

How did your movie, TV show, or song do? It had to get a checkmark on **EACH QUALITY** to be something God would really want you to watch. Otherwise, it's **possible** it was either sinful to watch or it is training your mind for sinfulness. It's that simple.

Even so, some girls still believe this lie.

LIE: "WHAT I WATCH/LISTEN TO DOESN'T MATTER."

Are you one of them? If you are, let me encourage you to talk to your mom or dad today. Tell them that you feel that God is asking you to be more careful about your entertainment choices and you'd like some help. I bet they'd be really happy you asked!

YOUR TURN IN THE LAB

Grab your pencils. It's your turn to do some work in our Truth Lab.

THE LIE	THE TRUTH
Sin isn't that big of a deal.	• **Sin separates us from God, no matter how big or small.** (Isaiah 59:2) • **If we confess our sin, God will forgive us.** (1 John 1:9)
I don't need to tell anyone about my sin.	• **Hiding your sin feels really bad.** • **You cannot overcome your sin and learn from it, if you don't get advice.** (Proverbs 28:13) • **The Bible tells you to confess your sins to someone.** (James 5:16) • **Only God can forgive you, but He is always faithful and fair and will forgive us when we confess to Him.** (1 John 1:9)
What I watch/listen to doesn't matter.	• **Everything we see or hear should be true, noble, right, pure, lovely, worthy of respect, excellent, and praiseworthy.** (Philippians 4:8)

TELLING MYSELF THE TRUTH

It's your turn to be the author!

- Have you believed any of these lies about sin? Put an X on top of any of **THE LIES** in this chapter that you have believed.
- What Truth do you need to think about **all the time**, **EVERY DAY**? Look at **THE TRUTH** we dug up together. Now circle what seems important for you personally to dwell on.
- Next, begin to think about it **all the time**, **EVERY DAY**. You can start by writing a prayer to God, a helpful Bible verse, or some ideas you don't want to forget in the space below.

Helping Zoey Believe Truth

It's time to give Zoey some advice!

What do you think? Should Zoey have a sleepover, and *not* invite Gigi? Why?

Lies about Being a Girl

"It's GREAT to be a girl!"

I shouted that today at recess when Gigi, Via, and I were going as fast as we could on the merry-go-round. Every day we try to see who can stay on the longest. It was **ME** today. Via gave up real quick, and Gigi went down next. We were laying on the ground, trying not to puke, when Via shouted, **"Girls RULE. Boys DROOOOL!"** Gigi said her mom doesn't let her say that because girls and boys are both important. That made Via mad. She asked Gigi, "Are you a girl hater?" Gigi said, "No! But why do you think boys have to be stupid for girls to feel smart?" Then, they had a big conversation that didn't make a lot of sense to me. They both say girls and boys aren't different, but how can Via say that AND believe "Girls Rule. Boys Drool"? SIGH! I'm super confused.

You aren't the only one, Zoey. It seems everyone, everywhere is talking about "Girls Rule. Boys Drool." They may not use those exact words, but they are trying to figure out if girls or boys are more important. Some are even trying to get rid of the differences between boys and girls.

Sometimes there are differences that are not good, and need to be changed. When I was a girl, many women did the same kind of work as men but got paid less than men. Now people have realized that's not okay, and are fighting to change things so men and women who have the same jobs and experience get paid the same. That's a good thing!

But sometimes the way people try to erase differences is not okay. While it is okay for a girl to dress more like a tomboy than a princess, she should also think, "It's great to be a girl." That doesn't mean she can't play basketball or work in construction, or that she can't like *Star Wars* more than *Cinderella*. It means that a girl shouldn't want to be so much like a boy that it erases everything about her that makes her girl-like. Doing that sends the message that being a girl isn't great at all.

Let's get right to an important Truth that you need to know about being a girl.

TRUTH #13 God created two different genders: male & female.

From the moment you were born (and even before that, according to Psalm 139:13–16), you were different from every boy ever born. Some things are obvious, but females and males are different in ways that you might not even see.

GIRLS & WOMEN

The bodies of most teen girls turn energy into a thicker layer of body fat, which gives them the ability to cushion and protect a baby one day. (This also makes them better at swim competitions, because their body stays warmer and works better in the water!)

Adult women have wider pelvis openings (which means their hips are more spread out and looser), giving them the ability to have babies in the future.

Women's brains tend to have more "wires" that connect thoughts, giving them the ability to do a lot of things at one time.

BOYS & MEN

The bodies of most teen boys turn energy into lean muscle, and by age 18, have 50% more muscle than most girls. This gives them more strength, and the ability to do harder physical work than most girls their age.[14]

Adult men have more compact pelvis structures (which means their hips are more tightly constructed and stronger). This gives them the ability to carry heavy things for longer periods of time without hurting themselves.[15]

Men's brains tend to have fewer and more direct "wires" to connect thoughts, giving them the ability to focus on one thing and be slow, thorough problem-solvers.[16]

Of course, there are still exceptions to everything in that chart. You just need to be the kind of girl God created you to be!

The point I'm making is this: It's true that girls and boys **can** both do **almost** anything. But their bodies, brains, and strengths generally have the word "different" written all over them.

Even so, a lot of people today believe this lie.

LIE: "BOYS AND GIRLS AREN'T REALLY THAT DIFFERENT."

Sometimes girls feel this way because they **do** like basketball or construction or *Star Wars*. Maybe they even want to "be strong like boys." (It's okay to work out and grow stronger, if that's something that's important to you.) Sometimes girls feel this way because they want to play football with their brothers or hunt with their dads. (It's okay to get out there and try things some other girls aren't doing!) Sometimes girls feel this way because they don't like the color pink or wearing dresses. (It's okay to love the color blue, and like wearing pants!) It's okay to be a different kind of girl.

But sometimes girls think boys and girls aren't different because they feel confused when someone they know is born a girl but **REALLY** wishes they were a boy. Is that okay? Let's look at a Bible verse to find an answer.

TRUTH NUGGET: **"Then God said, 'Let us make human beings in our image, to be like us. . . .' So God created human beings in his own image. In the image of God he created them; male and female he created them." (Genesis 1:26–27)**

You were created in God's "likeness." That means you were created to make people remember and think about God, because there are things about you that are like Him. **HOW COOL IS THAT?**

Grab two pencils. Circle the two words in our Truth Nugget that tell us what two specific things are mentioned about how we were created. I hope you circled the words **male** and **female**. Of course, there are a lot of things that make us like God. Our brains. Our creativity. But God only mentions **male** and **female** in this verse. So, being a girl must be a big deal. (So is being a boy. **That's why I don't really like sayings like, "Girls rule! Boys drool!"**)

It's because He wants us to look like Him. You might be wondering:

How does being a girl or a boy help us do THAT?

I'm glad you asked!

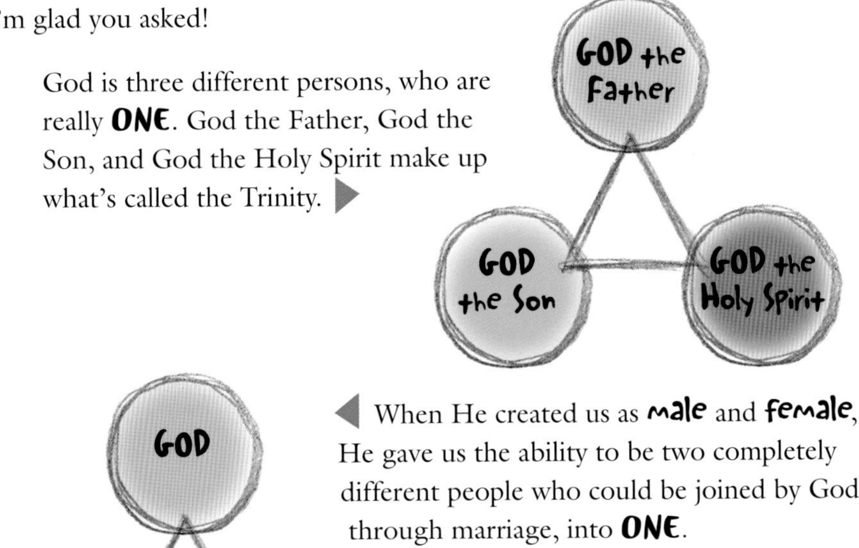

God is three different persons, who are really **ONE**. God the Father, God the Son, and God the Holy Spirit make up what's called the Trinity.

When He created us as **male** and **female**, He gave us the ability to be two completely different people who could be joined by God, through marriage, into **ONE**.

Does that mean you **have** to get married? No! But God created two genders. Male. Female. And it's important that you help to protect that Truth.

It's also important to say that you believe God created differences in females and males. This includes learning what the Bible teaches us about how we should interact with each other. It is important to know God's guidelines about how men and women were created so that we can live in this world the way that God planned.

This is one lie where the Bible chimes in loud and clear. It tells us that when someone decides to make up their own truth about males and females, they have "traded the truth about God for a lie" (Romans 1:25).

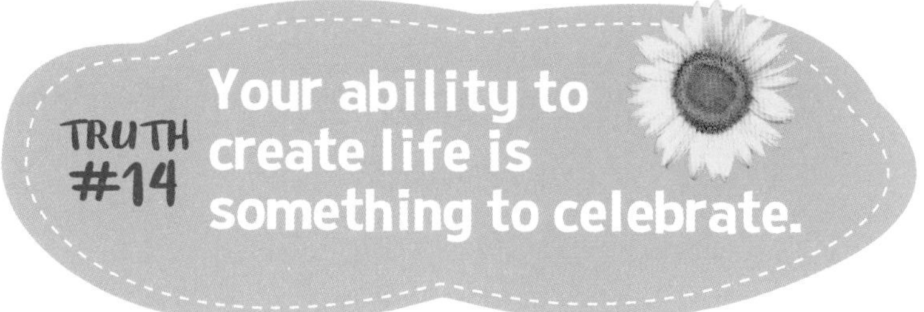

No one hands out awards, but every girl is going to change into a woman. This includes you! One of the biggest changes is getting your period. It happens anywhere between the ages of 9 and 16, so it's kinda hard to know exactly when it'll happen. The most noticeable sign will be some blood in your underwear. **Don't worry!** It's not because you're hurt, and it's totally normal. (Your mom, or grandma, or an auntie will help you learn more about how to take care of your body.)

Let me tell you what's really happening when you get your period. You have about 300,000 eggs in your body right now that could each become a full-out **HUMAN BEING**! (Relax! You're not going to have 300,000 babies.) Here's how it works:

- Each month some of these eggs are released from the part of your body called ovaries.
- A triangle shaped area called the uterus builds a nice, soft, cushiony lining so that **if** one or two of those eggs happens to begin to become a baby, there is a safe place to grow.
- But, if that doesn't happen, the uterus sheds its soft, cushy lining. This is what you see when you see blood.

WHAT IT LOOKS LIKE INSIDE YOUR BODY

Your period is all very scientific and amazing. The coolest thing is it reminds you that you are uniquely designed as a girl, and one of the special abilities of being female is the possibility of having babies one day. Here's what God says about becoming a mom:

TRUTH NUGGET: **"Children are a gift from the LORD; they are a reward from him."** (Psalm 127:3)

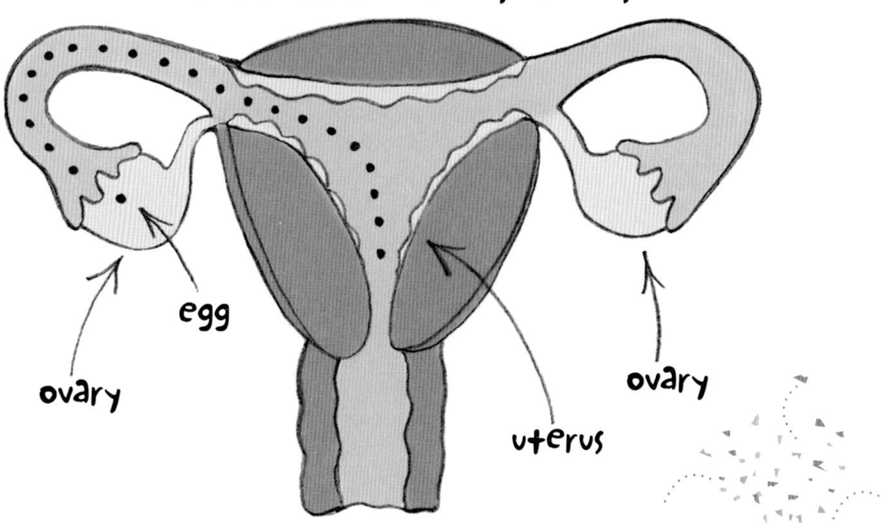

Having a body that is able to create babies is a good reason to **celebrate**! Some girls do something special when they start their period. Their moms take them out for a special dinner, or have a party where other women give them advice. I think that's a good idea.

But not everyone thinks getting their period is something to **celebrate**.

Some girls (and even some moms) believe this lie.

LIE: "GETTING MY PERIOD IS GOING TO BE AWFUL."

It is true that getting your period can be uncomfortable. Sometimes you have tummy cramps, or a headache. Some girls even get super moody and mean. (Don't do that! Having your period is not an excuse to be mean.) It's also true that having babies hurts. It is also wonderfully true that you generally forget the pain.

Trust me, getting your period is probably not going to be nearly as bad as you think. It's just new.

Something that has helped me respond well to my period is remembering that God wants us to do "everything" without "complaining." That includes getting your period. Remember that verse from Truth #6?

First Thessalonians 5:18 says "in everything give thanks" (NKJV). I find that anything hard becomes easier when I am thankful. Why not try telling God thanks for making you a girl instead of being nervous about your period? It's coming one way or another. You might as well have a good attitude about it.

Instead of dreading your period, kick off your womanhood with some **celebration**. It's not awful. It's actually awesome proof of your God-designed ability to have a baby, and it's worth **celebrating**.

YOUR TURN IN THE TRUTH LAB

Grab your pencils. It's your turn to dig deep.

THE LIE	THE TRUTH
Boys and girls aren't really different.	• **God created two different genders: male and female.** (Genesis 1:27) • **Girls and boys have a lot of physical, mental, and practical differences.** • **It's okay to be a different kind of girl, as long as you believe God made you to be a girl.** • **Those who do not believe in only two distinct genders—male and female— have traded God's Truth for a lie.** (Romans 1:25)
Getting my period is going to be awful.	• **Your period is awesome proof of your God-designed ability to have babies, and worth celebrating.** • **Having babies is a gift from God.** (Psalm 127:3, 5a) • **You should do everything—including getting your period—without grumbling or complaining.** (Philippians 2:14,16) • **You should do everything—including getting your period—with thanksgiving to God.** (1 Thessalonians 5:18)

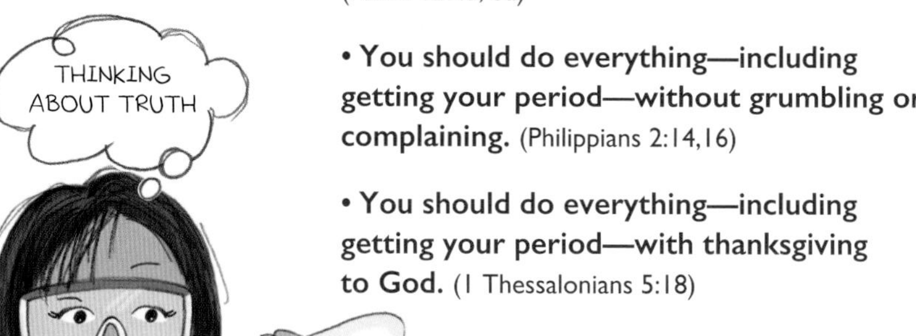

TELLING MYSELF THE TRUTH

It's your turn to be the author!

- Have you believed any of these lies about being a girl? Put an X on top of any of **THE LIES** in this chapter that you have believed.
- What Truth do you need to think about **all the time**, **EVERY DAY**? Look at **THE TRUTH** we dug up together. Now circle what seems important for you personally to dwell on.
- Next, begin to think about it **all the time**, **EVERY DAY**. You can start by writing a prayer to God, a helpful Bible verse, or some ideas you don't want to forget in the space below.

Helping Zoey Believe Truth

It's time to give Zoey some advice!

The conversation Zoey overheard at recess revealed that her friends are confused about the differences between boys and girls. Zoey got confused, too. Do you think it was okay for her friend to say, "Girls rule. Boys drool"? Why or why not?

Lies about Boys

In the history of forever, I have never made it through a trip to my Grandma Bing's house without **The QUESTION!** At Christmas this year, I thought I was going to get through, but **NO.** We actually had our coats on, and our Christmas bags all packed up. My lil' bro was even in his car seat. I hugged Grandma Bing, and then it happened: **"So, do you have a boyfriend yet?"** I slipped into the minivan as fast as I could, and I jumped into the back seat, managing not to explode from embarrassment. **Good grief!** She's been asking me that since **KINDERGARTEN!!!**

Has that ever happened to you? Sometimes it's not just kids your age who pressure you into being boy crazy. It seems some of the most trusted adults think it's funny to ask girls if they have a boyfriend.

If you don't think it's funny, you've come to the right place. I don't think it's funny either. Liking boys is serious business, because **LIKING BOYS** usually leads to wanting to be in special relationships with them. **Being in special relationships with BOYS** usually leads to dating them. And **DATING BOYS** usually leads to marrying one. Most people think marriage is pretty serious, so I think the topic of boys is pretty serious, too.

Here's a truth that a lot of you already know, because over half of the girls we talked to told us, "I plan to wait until I'm older to have a boyfriend."

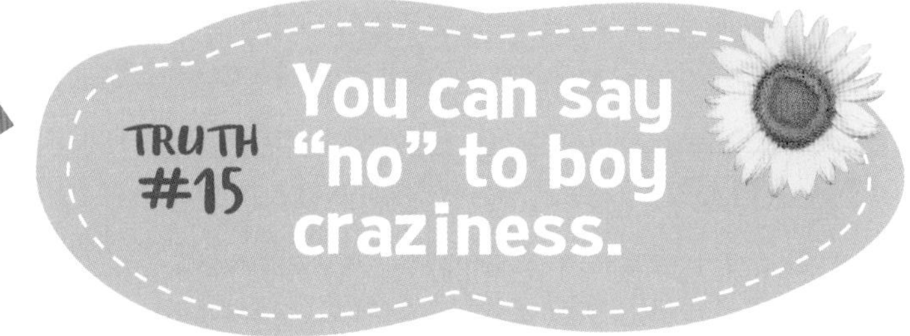

Maybe that sounds difficult to you. Even though a lot of girls didn't want to have a boyfriend yet, some of them already had one. So, I know you may feel some pressure.

You may even feel like you can't control the boy-crazy feelings you have. Maybe you believe that they're just feelings that naturally show up. Reminder: anytime you have a strong feeling, you need to check in with God's Truth to see how to respond to it. Here's a Truth Nugget that I hope will get some of you to jump off the boy-crazy train!

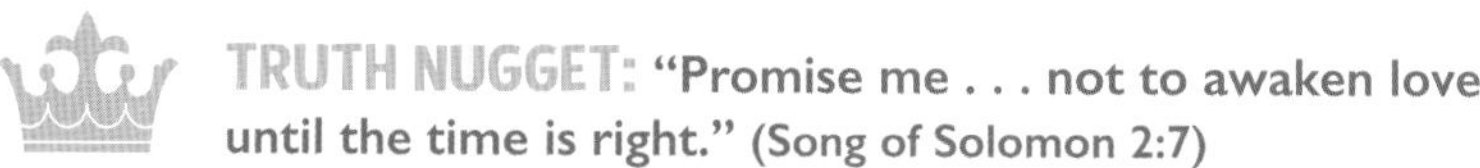

This verse is from the Bible's celebration of marriage and romantic love: Song of Solomon. The book says that both marriage and romance are good. It also gives helpful advice on how to experience love.

God designed marriage and love. He knows that feelings can overpower good choices, and that feelings aren't enough to support a relationship. This verse tells people of all ages not to get into a romantic relationship too soon, because it could grow faster than the commitment needed to make love last.

Are you ready to commit to someone for a lifetime? If the answer is no, this Bible verse applies to you. It's not the right time to "stir up" romantic love by being boy crazy.

Does that sound impossible in this boy-crazy world? God would not have put this verse in the Bible if it were **IMPOSSIBLE**! So, I know that you're able to say "no" to boy craziness. You may need to rely on God and others to help you, but it is possible.

Even so, some girls fall for this lie.

LIE: "IT'S OKAY TO BE BOY CRAZY."

21% of girls said it is okay to be boy crazy.

They told me it is "normal" to be boy crazy. Okay! Let me remind you once again: **normal is overrated!**

It's "normal" for some of your friends to be crazy about clothes and beauty products. But I can't find one place in the Bible where it says girls should be fashionable. I do find verses that say we should not be too concerned about those things.

It's "normal" for girls of all ages to have "frenemies"—friends who turn into enemies sometimes. And some say it's "normal" to be "mean girls." I can't find one place in the Bible where that's okay. Instead, I find verses that say things like this: **"Be kind to one another"** (Ephesians 4:32 NKJV).

It may also be "normal" for tween girls to be boy crazy, but it is not God's best. His word says you can wait, so I believe you're able to do that.

Do you know what kind of crazy you can be? God crazy! A God-crazy girl can be easily identified. She lets God have the first and last say in everything she does. That is to say, she obeys Him. Why not jump onto the God-crazy girl train with girls who believe, along with me, that they are able to wait for the right time to think about boys and love.

One way you can avoid being boy crazy is to talk to your mom. Or, she could help you jump off the boy-crazy train, if you're already on it. God gave you a mom to guide you. And the Bible says our parents should be the primary source of wisdom in all areas, including boys.

But this is where we have a super, ginormous, big problem to fix in the girl world.

80% of girls don't talk to their moms about boys.

Many of them say the reason is because it's weird.

Those girls are believing this lie.

LIE: "I DON'T NEED TO TALK TO MY MOM ABOUT BOYS."

GIRLS WHO BELIEVE THIS LIE SAID THINGS LIKE THIS:

- I'm not exactly comfortable talking about it with her.
- It's my personal secret. It's personal!

It may feel "weird." You might feel like you'll be losing some of your freedom and independence. (Remember, you **don't** need freedom. See page 69.) Maybe you have some fears that your mom might talk to other people about what you say, like maybe your dad. (Let me encourage you to talk to your mom about THAT, so she can understand your perspective.)

Once again, you need to check the Bible to know how to respond to your feelings. I want to encourage you to be stronger than your fears and do what God wants you to do: **talk with your mom**. How do I know He wants you to do that? Because this Truth Nugget says that we never outgrow the need for wise advice.

TRUTH NUGGET: "Walk with the wise and become wise; associate with fools and get in trouble." (Proverbs 13:20)

This Proverb is for you. It's for me. It's also for our moms and grandmas. It doesn't say "walk with wise people until you are 12, or 18, or 21." It just says to do it. You'll never outgrow this Bible verse.

"Walking with wise people" means including them in **all** areas of your life. That includes talking about boys. In fact, since marriage is such a big deal to God, the topic of boys may be one of the most important things to talk about.

Would it help you to know that your mom might feel a little uncomfortable about this too? For a long time, I have been helping moms and daughters talk about boys. (I believe it's **THAT** important!) One thing I recommend is starting a mother/daughter journal. This is a good way to ease into the more uncomfortable topics you need to talk about. (You can also use it with your grandma or auntie or a woman you like at church, if that's someone God has given you to talk to about important things!) It works like this:

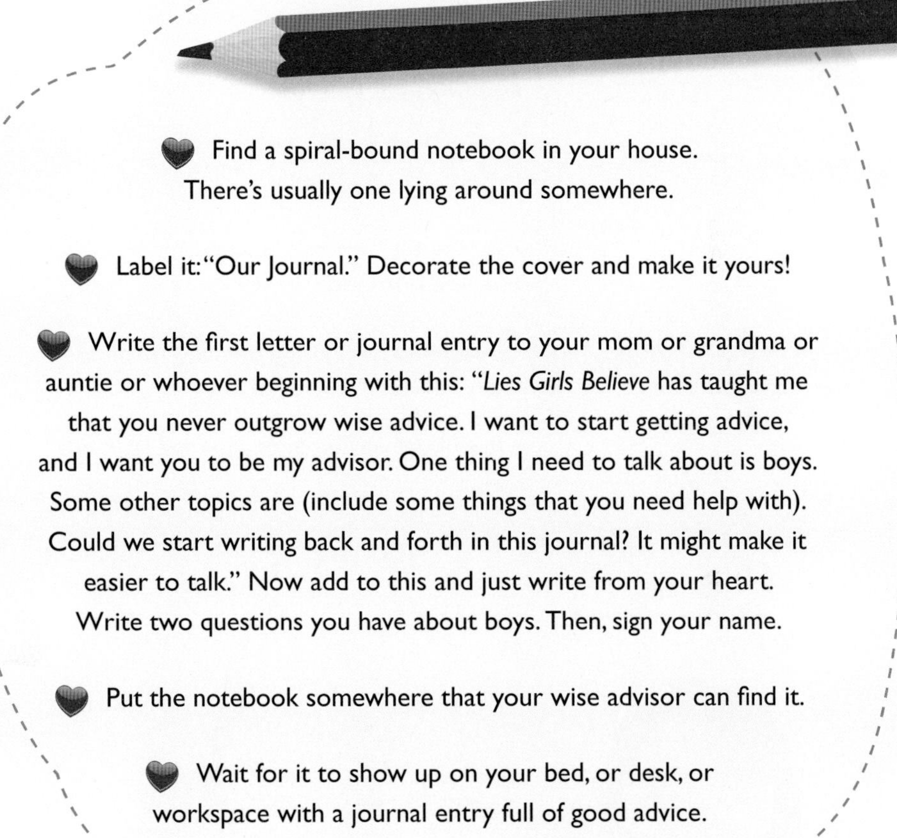

- Find a spiral-bound notebook in your house. There's usually one lying around somewhere.
- Label it: "Our Journal." Decorate the cover and make it yours!
- Write the first letter or journal entry to your mom or grandma or auntie or whoever beginning with this: "*Lies Girls Believe* has taught me that you never outgrow wise advice. I want to start getting advice, and I want you to be my advisor. One thing I need to talk about is boys. Some other topics are (include some things that you need help with). Could we start writing back and forth in this journal? It might make it easier to talk." Now add to this and just write from your heart. Write two questions you have about boys. Then, sign your name.
- Put the notebook somewhere that your wise advisor can find it.
- Wait for it to show up on your bed, or desk, or workspace with a journal entry full of good advice.

This has been a really good tool for some moms and daughters who have had a hard time getting started. And, I think you'll find that it gets easier once you dive in. One girl told me:

It's weird to talk to my mom about boys. But after you do it, you feel a lot better.

YOUR TURN IN THE LAB

Grab your pencils. It's your turn to dig deep.

THE LIE	THE TRUTH
It's okay to be boy crazy.	• **You should not "stir up" or "wake up" love until you can make a lifelong commitment to someone.** (Song of Solomon 2:7) • **It's better to be God crazy.** (2 Corinthians 5:13–14) • **It may be "normal" to be boy crazy, but it is not God's best.** (Philippians 2:15)
I don't need to talk to my mom about boys.	• **You will never outgrow the need for wise advice.** (Proverbs 13:20) • **It will get easier once you get started.**

TELLING MYSELF THE TRUTH

It's your turn to be the author!

- Have you believed any of these lies about boys? Put an X on top of any of THE LIES in this chapter that you have believed.
- What Truth do you need to think about **all the time**, EVERY DAY? Look at THE TRUTH we dug up together. Now circle what seems important for you personally to dwell on.
- Next, begin to think about it **all the time**, EVERY DAY. You can start by writing a prayer to God, a helpful Bible verse, or some ideas you don't want to forget in the space below.

Helping Zoey Believe Truth

It's time to give Zoey some advice!

How do you think Zoey should respond to her Grandma Bing the next time she asks if she has a boyfriend? (Hint: Maybe she should get some wise advice.) Do you think that Zoey should tell her mom that her grandma is making her feel awkward? How do you think Zoey could bring the topic up?

Lies about Friendship

I'm so **MAD AT GIGI. AGAIN!** She told me she "has no friends." Today at lunch, she told me she's going to sit with "Danika and them" from now on! Via and I sat alone. And Via had the guts to tell me that maybe I should worry less about how much I'm going to miss Gigi!!! She said that we should think about how we can help her, because she's worried about why she would do something like this.

Zoey is having a bad friend day. Have you ever had one of those? Not a surprise. Pretty much everyone in the girl world has had a bad friend day.

In fact, the stories in the Bible prove one thing about friendship. It's hard! Job's life was falling apart, and his three best friends made his pain even worse.[17] The first Christians fought so much that they decided not to work together, and started different ministries and churches.[18] Even two of Jesus' closest friends—Judas **and** Peter—were unfaithful to Him before He died![19]

If your friendships aren't perfect, join the rest of the world! There's no such thing as a perfect friend. But God wants us to keep learning. Even though the Bible reminds us that friendship can be difficult, it also offers us a lot of advice about how to do it well. One thing it tells us is this:

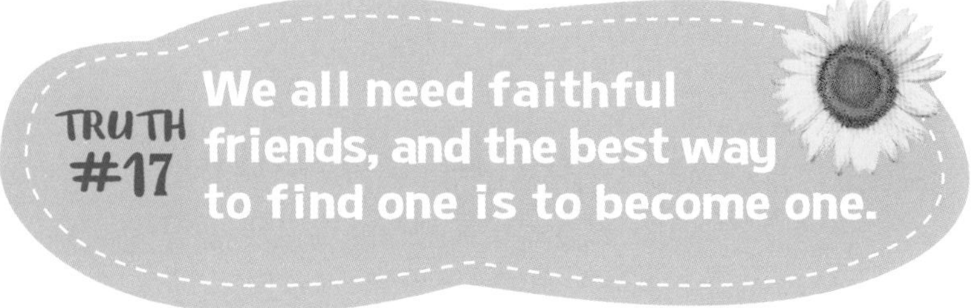

In an earlier chapter, we talked about how we were created to be a little bit like God. That is to say, we were created in His likeness or image. God the Father, God the Son, and God the Holy Spirit enjoy communicating with each other. You and I were created to be like that, too. So that desire you have for deep, real, true, amazing friendship is just another reminder that you were created to be like God. You need friendships, and were made to experience them.

That's why it makes me so sad when girls like you believe this lie.

LIE: "I DON'T HAVE ANY FRIENDS."

It may be true that you don't have a BFF that you hang out with, or that you aren't the most popular girl in your grade. It may be true that you just moved to a new place, and haven't met anyone yet. It may even be true that you've just had a bad friend day **TODAY**! But is it **really** true that you don't have **ANY** friends?

Before you answer that question, let me ask you another one: **what is a friend?** Obviously, a friend is someone you hang out with. The Bible has a lot to say about what makes someone a true friend. Here are five things it tells us are the differences between a frenemy—someone who is a friend one day and an enemy the next—and a true friend.

SIX FACTORS OF TRUE FRIENDSHIP

"FRENEMIES"

1. Love when it's convenient.

2. Hang around when it's good for them.

3. Lead others to make decisions that cause harm.

4. Want to be served.

5. Focus on self, and are bothered by the needs of others.

6. Say what others want to hear, no matter how true it is or is not. They'll maintain friends at any cost.

TRUE FRIENDS

1. Love all the time. (Proverbs 17:17)

2. Are loyal and faithful. (Proverbs 20:6)

3. Offer good advice that helps you make wise choices. (Proverbs 13:20)

4. Serve others. (John 15:13)

5. Focus on the needs of others. (Philippians 2:4)

6. Speak the Truth always, even when it's really hard and might risk the friendship. (Proverbs 27:6)

Now, I have another question: **when you read those things, were you asking yourself if you HAVE any friends like that OR were you wondering if you ARE a friend like that?**

Most of us tend to worry about if we **have** true friends, rather than being concerned about whether or not we **are** a true friend. Here's a Truth Nugget I still need quite often!

TRUTH NUGGET: "A man who has friends must himself be friendly, But there is a friend who sticks closer than a brother." (Proverbs 18:24 NKJV)

Wow! The Bible says that a person who has friends is one who has proven himself to be "friendly." In other words, they have the qualities of being a true friend. Are you a good friend?

This brings me to a really cool true story of friendship. Laura and Katrina grew up together since their moms were close friends. They had playdates since preschool.

In middle school, Katrina's parents got divorced and the girls' moms grew apart. Laura missed Katrina, but Katrina had started to be a real bully.

Laura got some good advice from her mom, and they prayed about it together. The next day Laura told Katrina, "I know you're going through a hard time. Is there anything I can do to help you? I'll do anything, but you **have** to be nice to me."

Laura was . . .

Katrina apologized. And today the girls are good friends again.

Rather than walking around saying, "I don't have any friends," maybe you could try looking around and asking God, "Who needs a friend?"

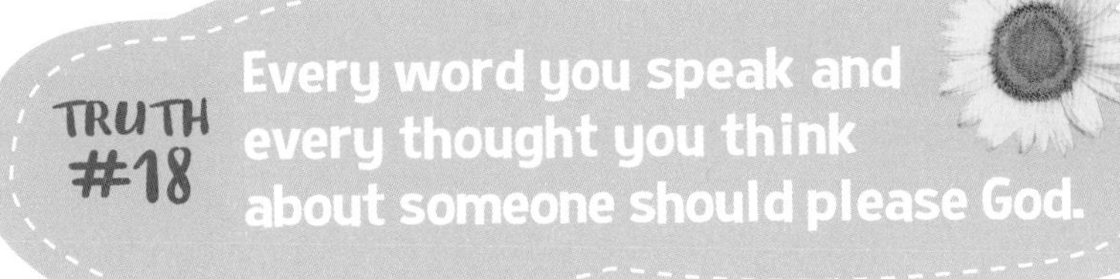

It's "normal" for girls of all ages—even MOMS—to have "frenemies" and occasionally to be "mean girls."

A lot of girls have experienced "mean girl" moments.

- Almost half of girls who took our survey say they have been bullied. (It's probably much higher than that in other surveys.)
- 29% of girls say they have been the bully or stood by and let it happen without doing anything to stop it.

Because it's so common,
a lot of girls believe this lie.

LIE: "IT'S OKAY TO BE MEAN."

Girls have always believed this lie. There are even stories in the Bible of adult women who treated each other really mean. (Sometimes girls don't outgrow being mean!) I think those stories made God really sad. I know it made the women sad, because the stories tell us so.

But, I think being mean is worse than ever. For one thing, girls use "mean girl talk" to greet each other! When they want to greet a good friend they haven't seen for a while, the might say something like, **"What's Up, Ugly???!!!"**

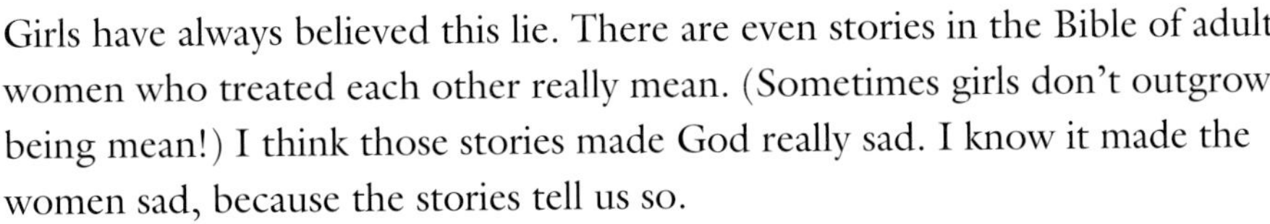

I CAN'T EVEN! STOP THE MADNESS!

Words have power. God created this earth with **WORDS**! And, if we are created in His image, our words have power too. Not as much power as His have, but still a lot.

I've never created a mountain or a star, but I have "created" friendship and courage and hope and faith with the words that I speak. I have also "created" anger and fear and sadness. Do you know what I mean? Have your words ever "created" bad feelings?

James 3 is about taming our tongues. It says that people have tamed all kinds of wild animals, birds, reptiles, and sea creatures, **BUT NO ONE CAN TAME THE TONGUE**!

Then, it reminds us that our tongues praise God, but still sometimes curse people. It says this shouldn't be how it is.

No, you can't tame your tongue, but do you know who can? God. And He has given us a lot of instruction in the Bible to help. Here's one of my favorite Truth Nuggets, because you can say it as a prayer to God.

TRUTH NUGGET: "May the words of my mouth and the meditation of my heart be pleasing to you, O LORD, my rock and redeemer." (Psalm 19:14)

If you call yourself a Christian and bless God with that tongue in your mouth, you should also use it to bless people. God hears every word you say to people, and knows every word you think about them.

That means, no more mean girls.

If you've been mean to someone like a friend or a sibling, this is a really good time to practice telling someone else about your sin. (See page 96.) Confess your "mean girl" moments to God and ask Him to forgive you. Then tell your mom. Ask her for help using words that are kind.

You know what else is important to talk about? If someone has been mean to you. Don't believe the lie that no one needs to know about it. And don't be embarrassed by it. **EVERYONE** has had moments when someone is mean to them. Could you do me a favor? Right now, I want you to go tell your mom or dad about the last time someone was mean to you. I'm pretty sure it'll make you feel a lot better! (It makes me feel better just thinking about it.)

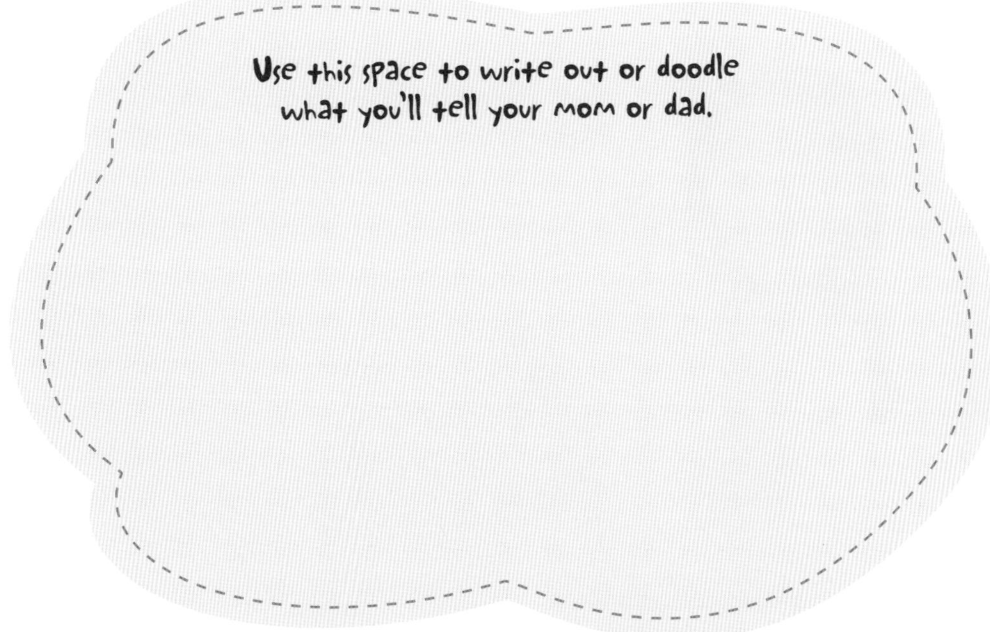

YOUR TURN IN THE LAB

Grab your pencils. It's your turn to dig deep.

THE LIE	THE TRUTH
I don't have any friends.	• You need to be less concerned about having friends, and more concerned about being a friend. • You need faithful friends, and the best way to find them is to become one. (Proverbs 18:24) • Friendship is difficult. Even Jesus (who was a perfect Friend) had problems in friendships. (Luke 22:47–62) • There are no perfect friendships.
It's okay to be mean.	• It's "normal" to be mean, but it's still sin. • God wants you to be kind. (Ephesians 4:32) • Words have power. (James 3:8) • You should not praise God with your tongue, and curse people with the same tongue. (James 3:10) • The words you say and the thoughts you think about others should be pleasing to God. (Psalm 19:14)

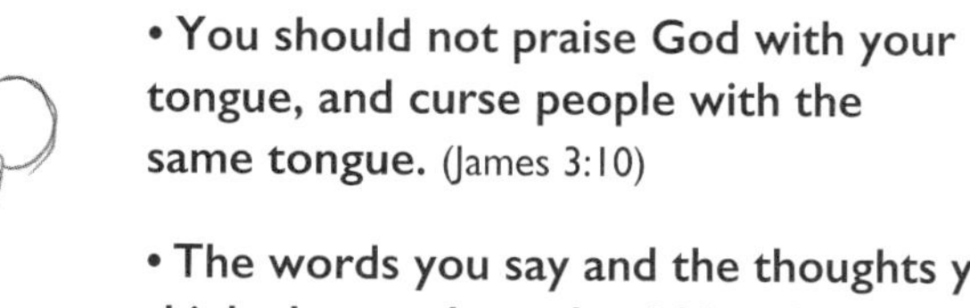

TELLING MYSELF THE TRUTH

It's your turn to be the author!

- Have you believed any of these lies about friendship? Put an X on top of any of **THE LIES** in this chapter that you have believed.
- What Truth do you need to think about **all the time**, **EVERY DAY**? Look at **THE TRUTH** we dug up together. Now circle what seems important for you personally to dwell on.
- Next, begin to think about it **all the time**, **EVERY DAY**. You can start by writing a prayer to God, a helpful Bible verse, or some ideas you don't want to forget in the space below.

Helping Zoey Believe Truth

It's time to give Zoey some advice!

Zoey has a decision to make. Will she take Via's advice and try to help Gigi? Should she? What would you tell her to do?

Lies about the Future

Today Danika told us she's going to go to **HARVARD UNIVERSITY**, and own an **important science lab** some day! A lot of people laughed at her, but I think it could be true. She is like the smartest girl in the whole class. Next thing I knew, Carly said something that made people laugh even louder. She said she wants to be a wife and a mom. Someone said, "Don't you know you're supposed to want more than **that**?!" I was secretly kind of sad, **but I don't know why.**

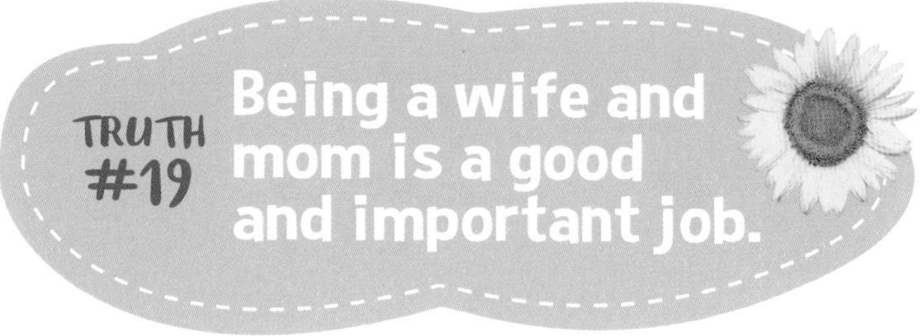

"What do you want to be when you grow up?"

That's a question people start asking you in preschool! Well, what **DO** you want to be when you grow up? **Write your top three choices below:**

1. ______________________________

2. ______________________________

3. ______________________________

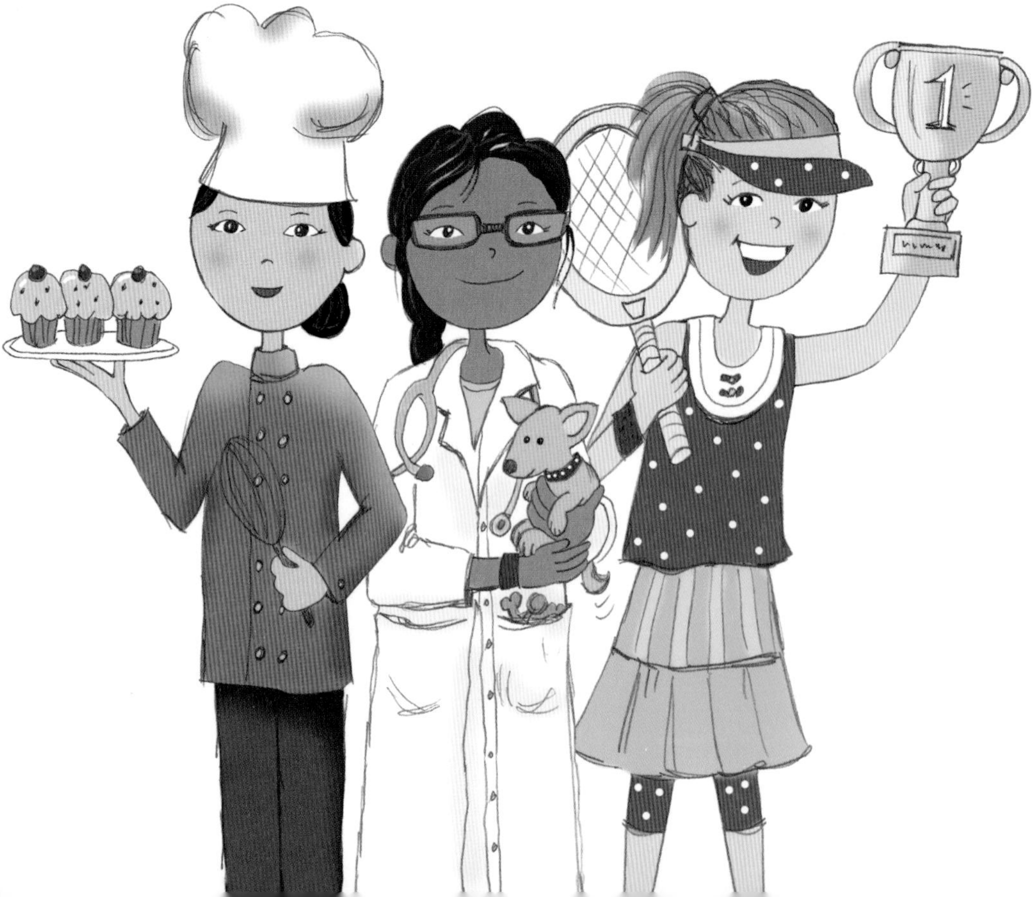

You are growing up at a very interesting time in history for women and girls. You can do almost **ANYTHING** you want when you grow up. It wasn't always like this. Can you believe that **way back in the day** women could not own property, vote, or even make as much money as men!!?? It's true.

The Bible tells us the stories of lots of women who did good work—for pay or for free to help people—outside of their homes. That tells me God could be planning a career outside of the home for you in the future.

But, there's a problem: a lot of girls are so obsessed with all they **WANT TO BE**, that they don't take time to ask God what they are **MEANT TO BE**! In fact, they think one of the best jobs God meant for women to love—being a wife and mom—just isn't **that** important. Some even think it's a bad idea to make it your goal in life!

They believe the lie:

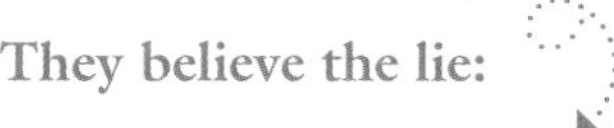

LIE: "IT'S NOT COOL TO BE JUST A WIFE AND A MOM."

I think this is a really big, bad lie, so I have two Nuggets of Truth for you. 

TRUTH NUGGET: "Then the LORD God said, 'It is not good for the man to be alone. I will make a helper who is just right for him.'" (Genesis 2:18)

This verse tells us why God created Eve. God didn't suddenly decide to make her at the last minute. He planned her all along. But first He wanted Adam to see that he needed someone with different qualities and strengths to help him. After that, God made Eve.

Some people think the word **helper** means Eve was not as important as Adam, but they don't understand this word! The book of Genesis was originally written in the Hebrew language and not in English. The word for helper was **ezer**. In this verse, it describes Eve as Adam's helper. But, in a lot of other Bible verses, this word describes **GOD AS OUR HELPER**! This is one of the cool ways that we, as women, get to be kind of like God. (Remember that from a few chapters ago? How we were made to be like Him?)

When you think of it **THAT** way, being a helper is super important. If you have a desire to be a wife one day, it is a good desire, and you can be proud of it. It is one of the best jobs God could ask you to do!

The second Truth Nugget I want you to see is this one. We have already used this Bible verse to fight another lie, but I think it's worth looking at again.

TRUTH NUGGET: "Children are a gift from the LORD; they are a reward from him." (Psalm 127:3)

Everyone likes to get gifts and be rewarded, right? In this verse, children are called a "gift" and a "reward." Even so, some women don't like the idea of being a mom. Even sadder to me, sometimes when they are moms, they complain about it a lot. They don't see it as a gift or reward.

This is a big lie in our world today, and one that I don't totally understand.

When I was a girl, there were three things I wanted to be when I grew up: a wife, a mom, and a Bible teacher. And I wanted them in that order! Even though I'm also a successful author, speaker, and Bible teacher—jobs I like a whole lot—the **BEST JOB EVER** has been being a wife and a mom.

Not every woman is **MEANT** to be a wife and mom, but most are. So, I hope you can be as excited about those jobs.

Here's what I think you need to do: tell God that you want to please Him with what you become in the future. Be willing to follow His plan. He created you and He knows what you were **MEANT TO BE**! If He wants you to be a wife and a mom, I'm sure you'll be a great one. He may also want you to have two careers, like me—and He will help you have wisdom about being a wife and mom, while you also grow into the responsibility of other things. Or maybe, you won't be married and become a mom at all because God has something else in mind for you.

I know one thing, He already knows and He is already preparing you. In fact, let's talk about our last big **TRUTH**!

TRUTH #20 You are becoming what you will be.

Does that truth sound confusing? Let me explain by telling you a story. When I first visited my friend Nancy's house, I noticed an interesting piece of framed art in her living room. It was a letter she wrote when she was 7 years old. It reads:

Dear Mommy & Daddy,

On Saturday, I knew that God had touched my heart and wanted me to be a missionary for Him, and it was just as if He had stood before me.

Right then I started to think . . . how a missionary would speak to people. I could just tell EVERYBODY this wonderful news. I'm so happy about it. And I just know that God has spoken to me and told me to be a missionary for Him. And I think being a missionary is the best job for me.

I'm just so happy that God wants me to be a missionary for Him.

Nancy

When Nancy was very young, she was already becoming what she is today: a great Bible teacher and an author who leads hundreds of thousands of women in growing closer to God. Her ministry, Revive Our Hearts, is now in many countries around the world. I think that makes her a missionary. The whole world over, women know her name and trust her. She didn't wait until she was an adult to start becoming a missionary. She started when she was 7!

This story illustrates this simple Truth of God.

TRUTH NUGGET: "Don't be misled—you cannot mock the justice of God. You will always harvest what you plant." (Galatians 6:7)

If you plant lima beans, what do you get? Lima beans! If you plant zucchini, what do you get? Zucchini!

This Bible verse tells us that the same sort of thing happens in our character. If you are a girl who reads the Bible and prays today, you are going to become a wise woman who loves God's Word and is a prayer warrior in the future.

But . . . if you are a girl who spends most of your time on the internet, playing computer games, or watching movies, it will be hard to grow a heart that loves to read the Bible and pray. Those things are not bad, and it's okay to enjoy them sometimes. But you also need to press into growing up and growing into what God hopes you will become one day. Whether that's a loving wife and mom, a lawyer, a pastor's wife, a doctor, a missionary, or a combination of all of the above!

This might be a good time for a little Note from Nancy.

Life can't be all fun. It's important to also focus on becoming what you will be when you grow up. That might mean practicing your piano, or learning to cook with your mom. It might mean studying your Bible, or working extra hard on your math homework. Before you do something, ask yourself this question: *What will that be worth in the long run?*

Does that sound too difficult and like it's something for older women to consider?

If so, you might be believing a lie.

LIE: "I'M TOO YOUNG TO ________________."

This lie shows up in a lot of different ways, to keep girls like you from planting good things in their lives. Sometimes it sounds like one of these lies.

- "I'm too young to read my Bible."
- "I'm too young to pray."
- "I'm too young to make my bed."
- "I'm too young to get up early."
- "I'm too young to save money."
- "I'm too young to give my heart to Christ and be a Christian."

If you are reading this book, you are not too young to do any of those things. Don't fall for the lie that what you are doing today as a tween girl doesn't really matter. It does. If you are disciplined, you will become disciplined. If you are kind, you will become kind. You are becoming what you will be.

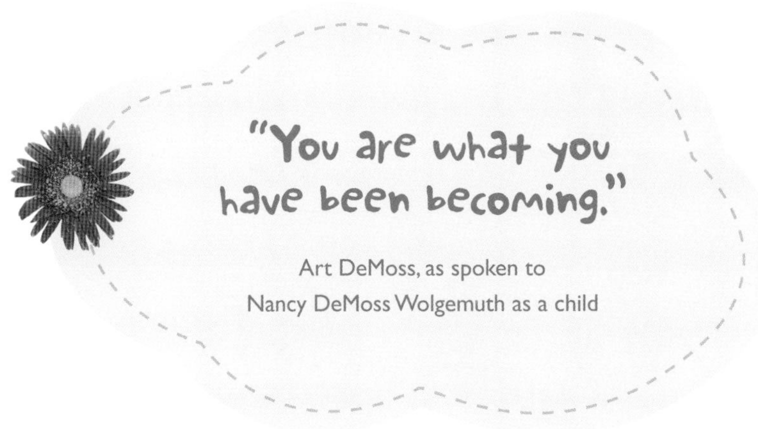

YOUR TURN IN THE LAB

Grab your pencils. It's your turn to dig deep.

THE LIE	THE TRUTH
It's not cool to want to be JUST a wife and mother.	• **God created the original woman, Eve, to be a helper for the original man, Adam. Every woman has this ability to help!** (Genesis 2:18) • **Children are a "gift" and a "reward."** (Psalm 127:3) • **It's okay to want to have a career outside of the home if that is what you are meant to have.**
I'm too young to ____________.	• **You are becoming what you will be. What you plant, you will harvest.** (Galatians 6:7)

TELLING MYSELF THE TRUTH

It's your turn to be the author!

- Have you believed any of these lies about the future? Put an X on top of any of **THE LIES** in this chapter that you have believed.
- What Truth do you need to think about **all the time**, **EVERY DAY**? Look at **THE TRUTH** we dug up together. Now circle what seems important for you personally to dwell on.
- Next, begin to think about it **all the time**, **EVERY DAY**. You can start by writing a prayer to God, a helpful Bible verse, or some ideas you don't want to forget in the space below.

Helping Zoey Believe Truth

It's time to give Zoey some advice!

Zoey watched people make fun of a girl who wanted to be a wife and mom. Do you think it is okay for that girl to want these things? Is there something Zoey could say to her friend to make her feel better?

the Truth That Sets You Free

what!? we're almost done with this book? NO!!!! I was waiting for you to get to a big question I have. Some of my friends say that the Bible has mistakes in it. They say it's out of style and old-fashioned. **It makes me feel really insecure and kind of sad** when I hear those things. **I think they might be believing lies**, but you didn't write about it. So, now what?!

Zoey, I'm so proud of you: you have discovered a lie by using your "sticky" emotions as evidence that it existed! The Truth is that the Bible is the most trustworthy book in existence. It's actually a collection of 66 books that were written by 40 different authors over a period of over 2,000 years.

You would think there would be a lot of different opinions on things. Many of the writers had different jobs and lived in different times and locations, but all of them recorded God's words and thoughts in such a way that they agree with each other. That's really rare in ancient documents.[20]

In fact, it would be pretty unbelievable for even two books written today to agree that much. But in the Bible, we have a miraculous agreement on topics!

A lot of people don't believe the Bible can be trusted because they don't want to obey the rules in it. They argue that it is out of style. **IT WAS NEVER IN STYLE!** The things that are written in it have always been radically unique for every culture in every period of time, including ours. God has always expected His people to be different than the rest of the world.

Zoey, you bring up a really good point: this book isn't big enough to include all of the lies every girl believes. There are as many different lies as there are different girls in the world. We only explored 20 of the common lies that girls believe. **So, what about the rest?**

In these last three chapters, I'm going to teach you how to identify lies and replace them with the Truth.

Your Thoughts Are the Boss of Your Feelings!

(How to recognize & identify lies)

I **cannot** stop thinking about the fact that **the Bible was never in style.** It's funny, but that makes me feel a lot better. I mean, I feel **less confused and more confident.** I thought for sure you were gonna tell me that the Bible **isn't** out of style. I guess the truth isn't always the opposite of a lie. **Doesn't that make it hard to figure out the truth? HELP!**

Yes, Zoey! You have to be careful when you're trying to figure out the Truth. **But don't worry!** The whole time you've been reading this book, you have been practicing how to recognize and identify lies, and to replace them with the Truth.

IT'S ALL ABOUT HOW YOU THINK!

No one is really sure of the exact number, but it's estimated that you think **2,000 TO 3,000** thoughts every single **HOUR**. What we do know is that these thoughts have the power to control how we feel. Cool, huh?!

Unless you have been thinking about lies! As you have learned, thinking about and believing lies makes you **feel** bad. Do you remember the last time you felt really down? I bet you were thinking negative thoughts about yourself. Things like, **"I don't have any friends."** Or **"I'm the dumbest person alive!"** Or **"My life stinks."**

If you're not careful, your brain starts to believe what you think about **even if it's not true!** This is something God has been trying to teach us for a long, long time. Even before Jesus was born, the Bible communicated this Truth.

TRUTH NUGGET: "As he thinks in his heart, so is he." (Proverbs 23:7 NKJV)

Here's the good news: you can actually change the way you feel by changing what you think about. **Your thoughts are the boss of your feelings.**

In these last two chapters, I'll show you three steps to help you control your feelings by controlling your thoughts. **And you do that by believing the Truth.**

Let's get started!

HOW TO **REPLACE A LIE WITH THE TRUTH**

1. **Recognize the evidence.** (Look for any sin or "sticky" feelings.)

2. **Identify the lie and stop feeding it.** (Make a commitment to stop thinking about it so much.)

3. **Replace the lie with the Truth.** (Find verses in the Bible to help you think about the Truth.)

RECOGNIZE THE EVIDENCE

Remember, lies always make us feel controlled, unhappy, and trapped.

When we first met Zoey, she was obsessed with an app and thought about it **all the time**, **EVERY DAY**. She listened to friends who told her that she **really** needed it to stay connected with them. This made her feel more and more **insecure and left out**. Because of this, she was already in trouble. She was trapped! Her parents said she was not ready for this app. **She disobeyed her parents** and secretly downloaded it anyway. It didn't make her feel better, but much worse. She **felt embarrassed and disappointed** in herself for doing it. She was even more trapped.

 **Stop right there!**

It's time to think super hard again . . . but this time, we're going to need a shovel to dig in the dirt! You see, a lie is like the root of a weed and I want you to dig it up so it can't grow.

Have you ever ripped up a weed by the roots? It's easy if the seed has just begun to grow and the root is tender, but sometimes I have to take shovels and axes to weeds that have grown for a long time in my garden. Roots can be deep and strong. But the roots of all lies have to be dug up!

But wait! You have to dig in the right place. Sometimes lies are difficult to detect.

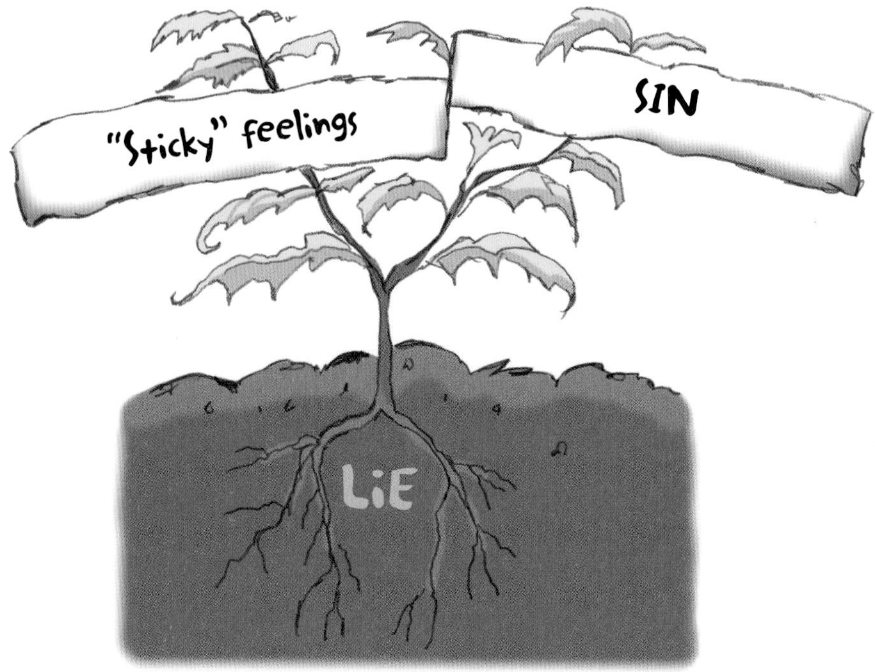

Our first task is to **identify the evidence** that reveals a lie under the surface. There are two kinds of evidence we see above the ground: "**sticky**" **feelings** and **sin**. Sometimes you see only one, but often we can see both.

Let's stop and identify the evidence of a lie in Zoey's life. Look at the paragraph in blue on the previous page that summarizes her experience with the app.

Circle the sin Zoey committed.

Put a box around the "sticky" emotions that she felt both before and after her sin. Remember how we learned that some emotions don't simply come, do their job, and then leave? They stick to us, and we end up thinking about them **all the time**, **EVERY DAY**.

Now begin to label the illustration below by writing in the "sticky" emotions and sin that are the evidence of Zoey's lie. These are the things we can easily see.

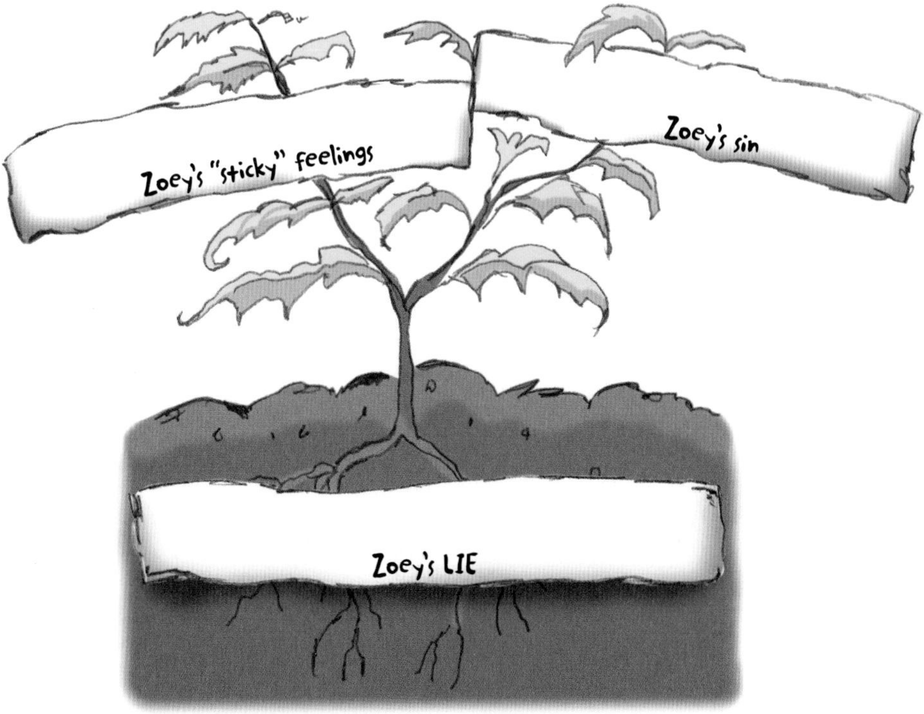

Zoey's "sticky" feelings

Zoey's sin

Zoey's LIE

Zoe started by feeling **insecure** and **left out**. This resulted in the sin of **disobeying her parents**. Zoey's lie was **my life would be better with that app**. That was followed by more "sticky" emotions.

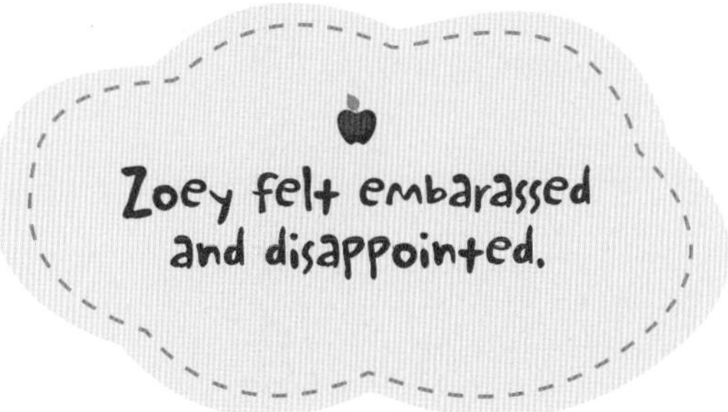

Now, let's talk about Y-O-U! Are you struggling with any "sticky" feelings that won't go away? Are there any sins you have committed lately, or maybe a long time ago, but you can't stop thinking about them? Or do you have a strong desire to sin?

Fill in the blanks below to see if there is any evidence above the surface that you might have the root of a lie growing deep down inside of you.

- **SOME "STICKY" FEELINGS** I'm having lately include:

  ____

  ____

  ____

- **A SIN** I committed recently or can't stop thinking about is:

  ____

  ____

  ____

- **A DESIRE TO SIN** I'm facing a lot is: ______________

  ____

  ____

  ____

IDENTIFY THE LIE & STOP FEEDING IT

We're going to use what you just wrote to identify a lie you are believing. Then I'm going to teach you how to keep it from growing stronger in your heart and mind.

It can be difficult to identify a lie. They're under the surface and hard to see. I usually need help from a friend, and you will too. So, ask your mom or an adult you trust to help you with this next section. Go ahead! Go get them now.

Let's look at Zoey's lie one more time.

ZOEY'S BIG LIE:
"My life would be better with that app."

Write her lie on the illustration on page 145.
Write her lie on the illustration on page 145.

Was her life better? Nope! She ended up with more bad emotions and lies. It was not true at all.

NOW, LET'S TALK ABOUT YOU AGAIN!

Look back at the "sticky" emotions, sin, or desire to sin that you wrote about on the previous page. Pray and ask God to help you to see what the root lie is under the evidence. (Remember, it's a really good idea to have some help with this! I hope you grabbed someone.)

Take your time.
Get advice.
Think hard!
Pray hard!
Got it?

A LIE I am believing is:

Good work!

You've identified your first lie.
Now, all you have to do is **STOP FEEDING IT!**
But, I know that is hard sometimes!

Zoey spent a lot of time dwelling on or feeding her lie, and I bet you have too. Most people end up thinking about lies **all the time**, **EVERY DAY**. Thoughts are like fertilizer and water for the roots growing inside our minds. They feed them.

Let's say I plant two seeds in the ground, but I only fertilize and water one of them. **Which one will grow faster?**

The one I feed, right?

You have to stop feeding a lie. The way you stop feeding a lie is by forcing yourself to stop thinking about it. Sometimes that means you have to stop exposing yourself to the lie.

For Zoey, this may have meant giving her tablet to her mom, or maybe just telling her friend to stop talking about the app because she wasn't allowed to have it. For a girl who is bothered by lies about how she looks, it may mean looking in the mirror a few less times a day. For a girl who worries about being the very best on her favorite team, it may mean putting the ball on a shelf for a short time. For a girl who is boy crazy, it might mean making a simple decision not to get into a relationship until a certain age.

You see? The key is thinking about the lie less.

By doing this, you not only stop feeding the lie, but you are also able to rip up the root of it.

How will you stop feeding your lie so you can tear it out? Ask for advice from your mom or the adult you got to help you, and then doodle and write about how you're going to rip up the root of the lie!

Hold tight! You're not finished yet. You see that big empty space that the lie left behind? We have to fill it up with something. It's time for the best part!

Let's replace the lie with God's Truth in the next chapter.

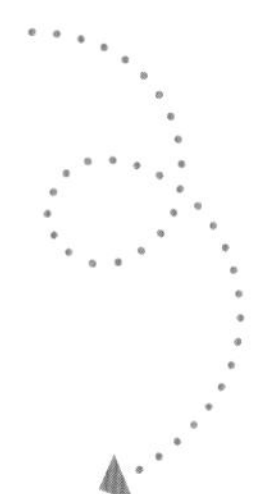

CHAPTER 13

Jesus Wants to Be the Boss of Your Thoughts!

(How to replace lies with the Truth)

I get it! I'm going to stop thinking about the apps everyone else has. And, Dannah, that friend really isn't good for me, so I need to stop hanging out with her. That'll make sure my thoughts don't plant that lie in my mind again. **This is GREAT!**

Yep, but Zoey, there's one more step to overcoming lies. It's time for you to make a big, important life decision. If your thoughts are the boss of your feelings, **who or what is going to be the boss of your thoughts?**

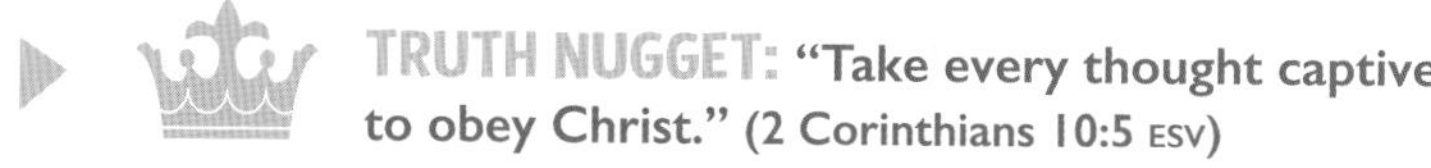

TRUTH NUGGET: "Take every thought captive to obey Christ." (2 Corinthians 10:5 ESV)

Jesus Christ wants to be the boss of every thought you have. He can be. But it's up to you. Will you let Him?

Maybe the best way to show you how this works is to tell you how I did it the week I wrote this chapter. I was in the Dominican Republic where I did four events for girls your age. What great fun we had worshipping God, playing games, and studying the Truth.

However, it wasn't always easy. When I got really tired, I began to lose control of my thoughts. I was backstage in Santo Domingo where a lot of my friends had come to see the event, and I was feeling a lot of bad emotions **all at the same time**!

I recognized the evidence of a lie:
I felt very **afraid** and **insecure**.

There were a lot of "sticky" feelings that I was letting stick to me! Here are some of the thoughts that were bothering me: **My friends aren't going to have any fun. They're going to leave early. I'm not a good Bible teacher. If they don't like the event, they won't like me.**

I identified the lie:
I **NEED** their approval!

So, I ripped that lie up by its roots by helping people who were backstage at the event. (Sometimes being busy takes your mind off of "sticky" feelings.) Then, when I was alone, I said this simple prayer: "Jesus, You are in charge of my thoughts. I want them to be obedient to You! Help me to replace this lie with Your Truth. Take control. My thoughts belong to You, and You get to be in charge of them."

Immediately, Jesus brought a Bible verse to my mind to replace that lie with His Truth. It was this one:

TRUTH NUGGET: "For am I now seeking the approval of man, or of God? Or am I trying to please man? If I were still trying to please man, I would not be a servant of Christ." (Galatians 1:10 ESV)

God's Truth is that I do not need the approval of my friends; I only need to seek to please Him. When I worry about what others think, I'm focused on pleasing the wrong person. In this case, the Truth I needed was the opposite of my lie.

I identified the Truth:
I **NEED GOD'S** approval!
I'm **HIS** servant!

I began to think about this Truth over and over. By doing so, **I replaced the lie with God's Truth**! And you know what? That night people told me I taught with a special strength in my words. The best news is that 58 girls said they wanted to become Christians that night! (Trust me, that doesn't happen very often. In fact, I think it might be the most in one night at one of my events.) **And it felt great to know that I was letting Jesus be the boss of my thoughts. That way, He could let me be a part of what He was doing in the hearts of those girls!**

You have a big decision to make at the end: **Who or what is going to be the boss of YOUR thoughts?** Will you let Jesus have control? Will you choose to make your thoughts line up with God's Truth? Let's try it with the lie you identified in the last chapter. Look at it again on page 147.

Now, there are a lot of ways you can find the Truth to replace the lie. **Here are three ideas.**

3 WAYS TO FIND BIBLE VERSES TO REVEAL GOD'S TRUTH

1. **Pray and ask God to bring to your mind** a verse you have memorized, or have heard before.
2. **Ask an adult you know who is a Christian** to help. Maybe your mom, dad, grandma, or grandpa can think of a Bible verse.
3. **If your parents are okay with you using the Internet**, use an online Bible search engine such as biblegateway.com. Look up a keyword in your lie. For example, my keyword would be "approval." If I used a concordance to search for verses that had that word, I would have discovered Galatians 1:10, along with a lot of other helpful verses.

Once you find the Truth to replace your lie, it's a good idea to write it on a piece of paper or a notecard and put it somewhere that you can see it every day.

The goal is to think about God's Truth **all the time**, **EVERY DAY**! That is how you rip up a lie by the root, and replace it with God's Truth! Remember that big hole a lie leaves when you rip it up? Well, it has to be filled with something. This is your chance to plant truth.

Let me tell you how a girl named Kelly actually did this in her life. Third grade was really difficult for her. She was a slow reader and writer, and had a teacher who was impatient with her. Before long, Kelly developed a fear of school. In the morning, she checked her backpack six to eight times before leaving the house, terrified that she'd forgotten something and would make her teacher even more impatient. By the time fourth grade rolled around, Kelly was a mess!

Kelly's mom and dad never stopped praying and believing God was teaching their daughter something important. But sometimes they had to physically pick her up and put her in the car to go to school. Through the advice of a Christian counselor, Kelly started replacing her anxious thoughts with Bible verses. She actually started to write words from the Bible back to God as prayers in her journal. She has a whole book full of evidence that she is **a girl who has chosen to let Jesus and His Word be the boss of her thoughts!**

Today, Kelly is in sixth grade. She is still a slow writer and reader, but she is also confident that she is loved and valued by God. Because she allowed Jesus to be in control of her thoughts, she is no longer fearful of school. Instead, she faces each day with joy and excitement.

Kelly's story proves that replacing lies with the Truth takes time. (It took her almost a full year!) You need to keep finding new Truth, memorizing verses, and reviewing them regularly. (I actually have a little spiral bound stack of notecards with handwritten Truth that I carry in my purse.) But, oh, the life of freedom God has for you is every bit worth the hard work!

TOP 10 PLACES to Post Bible Verses When You're Overcoming Lies

10 Your bedroom door so you see them every time you go in.

9 The back cover of your Bible.

8 Your lunch box, if you're still a packer.

7 Your mom's purse . . . for drastic emergencies.

6 Your best friend's bedroom, so she can read them to you.

5 Your locker, if you have one.

4 Your bathroom mirror.

3 The headboard of your bed.

2 On your computer.

1 Above the doorway of your bedroom so you see them every time you leave.

Wear the Belt of Truth

(Using Truth to be set free)

Is this really the last chapter!? **NOOOOO!!!** I'm just starting to get the hang of identifying lies and believing Truth. I feel so FREE! And I like how I feel. But now you're leaving me, and I'm kinda freakin' out! I don't want to go back to believing lies, because I sure didn't like how they made me feel. Is there any way to avoid it forever and ever?

Like Zoey, I wish there was a way to avoid ever feeling "sticky" emotions. But sometimes **I** still struggle with them, and if I'm not careful that leads me to believe lies. Everyone struggles. As long as we live, we have to do the hard work of identifying lies, ripping them up, and replacing them with Truth.

Do you feel the same way as Zoey?

I have some really good news! I have discovered one simple thing that helps me avoid the lies and live in the Truth. It's as easy as getting dressed in the morning.

Every day you wake up and put on clothes, right? Well, living in Truth is kind of like that. You have to put it on **EVERY DAY**. I want you to learn to wear Truth!

Lots of Bible verses tell us to "put on" things, like humility, righteousness, and love. Sure, you don't actually put your arms through it and put it on your body, but maybe you think to yourself: "I'm going to pick up the Truth today and wear it! I'm going to cover myself with kindness and love."

These things are spiritual characteristics that can be worn just like a pair of your favorite jeans or a team jersey! (You can't touch them or feel them, but I think you can kind of "see" when someone wears those things!) One of the things we can "put on" is the belt of Truth.

TRUTH NUGGET: "Stand up and do not be moved. Wear a belt of truth around your body." (Ephesians 6:14 NLV)

When the apostle Paul wrote this Bible verse, he also encouraged Christians to wear a bunch of other stuff like:

- **the shield of righteousness**
- **shoes of peace**
- **the helmet of salvation**
- **the shield of faith**
- **the sword of the Spirit, or the Word of God**

We call all these things the armor of God, and they're all important for Christians to "put on." But the "belt of Truth" is the **very first** thing Paul mentions. Why?

Well, back when Paul wrote the verses, Roman soldiers wore a belt that was a lot different from the simple leather straps we wear today.

It was a thick, heavy band made out of leather and metal, with a big protective piece that hung down in the front of it. The belt held the soldier's sword and other weapons in place.

YOUR belt of Truth holds everything else in place too. It helps you make right choices. It keeps you living in peace. It helps you keep your faith. You get the idea!!! You **have** to put it on to keep the other stuff in place.

How do you do that?

I'm glad you asked. The answer is pretty simple.

I like to do this first thing in the morning by reading my Bible and writing verses in a journal. You may find a favorite devotional book you enjoy, or maybe you'd rather have family devotions or mother/daughter devos. Maybe you will start a collection of your favorite Bible verses and tape them to your bedroom wall. It doesn't matter how you do it, but get into the Bible every single day! Each time you do, you are "putting on" the very important belt of Truth.

In this final chapter, I'm going to help you "put on" the belt of Truth. On the next four pages is a list of 20 key Truths. You'll recognize them. They come from the topics we studied together. Review this list and use it often, my friend. Take time to look up the Bible verses next to different Truths as you focus on them. You may even want to write out these Truths and verses in your journal. I believe you are going to be a strong and mighty girl who stands for Truth!

20 KEY TRUTHS

You could cut these pages out and post them in your bedroom, or write the Truths in a journal.

1. When you feel like God might not love you.

TRUTH: God loves you **all the time**, **EVERY DAY**, even when you have done something bad. He doesn't want you to sin and hurt because of it, but He loves you no matter what and is always ready to forgive you. (*Romans 5:8*)

2. When you feel like God is not enough.

TRUTH: God is all you need. He is more important than friends or grades or stuff because He is the source of everything you need. (*Philippians 4:19*)

3. When you aren't sure if you are a Christian or not.

TRUTH: You are a Christian if you have "confessed with your mouth that Jesus is Lord and you believe in your heart that God raised Him from the dead" (*Romans 10:9*). And you will be different, because becoming a Christian changes the way you act. You want more of God and less of this world. (*2 Corinthians 5:17; 1 John 2:3–17*)

4. When you don't feel like you are good enough.

TRUTH: No matter how you perform or who likes you or who doesn't like you, if you are a Christian, you have been chosen by God. On our own, we are not good enough, but with Him we are enough. (*Ephesians 1:4*)

5. When you feel fat or ugly, and feel like pretty girls are worth more.

TRUTH: God made you, and you are perfectly made. He didn't make any mistakes when He made you. But He is a lot less concerned with the outside of you than you are. The beauty He sees is on the inside of you and shows up as things like kindness, helpfulness, and gentleness. (*1 Samuel 16:7*)

6. When you feel like you don't have enough freedom.

TRUTH: You don't need more freedom. You are ready for more responsibility, and God wants you to step into that. (*Galatians 6:5–6*)

7. When you feel like your family is weird.

TRUTH: Remember that different is good. Your family is different. Every family is, and that's good. God doesn't want us to be like everyone else, but to be different because we are obeying Him. (*Ephesians 4:17, 19–20*)

8. When you feel like your family is too broken for you to be happy.

TRUTH: God, not your family, is the source of everything. He wants to be the source of your contentment. He will teach you how to trust Him and be content in the family that you have.* (*Philippians 4:11–12*)

* There are some important exceptions to being content. If someone is hurting you, touching you in ways that make you feel uncomfortable, or saying a lot of cruel things to you, TELL SOMEONE! That is called abuse, and you should never be content with it.

9. When you feel like your parents don't "get" you.

TRUTH: While it's great to get along with your parents and enjoy spending time with them, they aren't supposed to be your friends, but your parents. It's their job to set boundaries. It's your job to obey them. God will give you joy when you choose to honor your parents. (And when you're older, there's a good chance you and they will become great friends!) (*Ephesians 6:1–2*)

10. When you are tempted to believe that your sin is no big deal.

TRUTH: All sin separates us from God, and sometimes from other people we know and love. (*Isaiah 59:2*)

11. When you are tempted to believe you don't need to tell anyone about your sin.

TRUTH: Remember that hiding your sin sets you up for failure. You need help overcoming bad habits, temptations, and sin. Ask someone older and wiser for help. (*Proverbs 28:13; James 5:16*)

12. When you think you can watch any movie or TV show, and listen to any music you want without it impacting you.

TRUTH: What we watch, listen to, and read changes us. It makes us believe and behave differently. God wants us to only expose ourselves to things that are true, noble, right, pure, lovely, and worthy of praise. (*Philippians 4:8*)

13. When it seems like boys and girls aren't all that different.

TRUTH: God created two genders: male and female. They are important because they help us understand who God is, and that He is a social being. It is good to celebrate and understand the differences between boys and girls. (*Genesis 1:26–27*)

14. When you are afraid of getting your period.

TRUTH: It's not going to be nearly as bad as you think. Every girl gets one. The best thing you can do is talk to your mom about it so you're prepared, and remember that it's a sign that your body has the ability to create life. Be thankful for this gift. (*Psalm 127:3*)

15. When everyone around you is boy crazy and you feel tempted to be.

TRUTH: It may be "normal" to be boy crazy, but it is not God's best for you. You can say no to boy craziness. (*Song of Solomon 2:7*)

16. When you believe the lie that you don't need to talk to your mom about boys.

TRUTH: It may be uncomfortable sometimes, but you should talk to your mom, or another trusted adult, about boys. Getting married one day, if that's what God wants for you, is a really important thing. So, talking to your mom about boys is too. Everyone needs wise advice. (*Proverbs 13:20*)

17. When you feel like you don't have any friends.

TRUTH: We all need faithful friends, and the best way to find one is to become one. Think about how you can be a good friend, and look for people who need one. (*Proverbs 18:24*)

18. When you are struggling with being mean.

TRUTH: Every word you speak and every thought you think about someone should please God. It may be normal to be mean, but God wants you to be kind to everyone. (*Psalm 19:14*)

19. When you think having a big career is more important than being a wife and mom, if that is what God has planned for you.

TRUTH: It is a cool thing to be able to help a husband. Being a mom is one of the best gifts you'll ever get (*Genesis 2:18; Psalm 127:3*)

20. When you think you are too young to start doing mature things.

TRUTH: You are becoming who you are. If you are being kind, you will become kind. If you are being a wise girl, you will become a wise woman. (*Galatians 6:7*)

I hope you'll use this list of Truths to "put on" the belt of Truth each day. Wear Truth! Let people see it all over you in the way you act, because the way you act is controlled by Truth, not "sticky" emotions! I'm praying for you!

NOTES

1. James 5:19–20.

2. Dictionary.com Unabridged, based on the Random House Unabridged Dictionary, © Random House, Inc. 2018, s.v. "lie," http://www.dictionary.com/browse/lie/.

3. Amanda MacMillan, "Why Instagram Is the Worst Social Media for Mental Health," *Time,* May 25, 2017, http://time.com/4793331/instagram-social-media-mental-health/.

4. This definition of "bondage" is a simplified version based on definitions found at Dictionary.com Unabridged, based on the Random House Unabridged Dictionary, © Random House, Inc. 2018, s.v. "bondage," http://www.dictionary.com/browse/bondage.

5. Dictionary.com Unabridged, based on the Random House Unabridged Dictionary, © Random House, Inc. 2018, s.v. "truth," http://www.dictionary.com/browse/truth?s=t

6. This concept is updated and simplified from Philip Yancey, *Rumors of Another World* (Grand Rapids: Zondervan, 2003), 144.

7. Philip Yancey, *What's So Amazing About Grace* (Grand Rapids: Zondervan, 2002), 70.

8. This represents our survey which involved 1,531 "churched" girls between the ages of 7–12. Some surveys that included both "churched" and "unchurched" girls found that a much higher percentage of girls did not like how they look.

9. Sadie Robertson's Facebook page, accessed January 2, 2018, https://www.facebook.com/sadiecrobertson/posts/707756299425971:0.

10. "What Is Responsibility?," TalkingTreeBooks.com, accessed January 4, 2018, https://talkingtreebooks.com/definition/what-is-responsibility.html.

11. The word tween first made a debut in 1941, despite the fact that it was not widely used until more recently. Prior to that, the word preteen made an appearance in the 1920's. Both were words created by people who wanted to sell new products to that age group. https://blog.oxford-dictionaries.com/2015/01/13/tweens-teens-twentysomethings-history-words-young-people/, retrieved February 19, 2018.

12. Google Dictionary, s.v. "content."

13. Nancy DeMoss Wolgemuth, *Lies Women Believe: And the Truth That Sets Them Free* (Chicago: Moody Publishers, 2018), 98–99. This quote has been modified by permission of the publisher to accommodate the reading level of *Lies Girls Believe*, but remains the same in essence.

14. Alfred Gluckman, *Sexual Dismorphism in Human and Mammalian Biology and Pathology* (Cambridge, MA: Academic Press, 1981), 66–75.

15. Igor Klibanov, "Key Structural Differences Between Men and Women," *Fitness Solutions* (blog), February 23, 2016, https://www.fitnesssolutions plus.ca/blog/key-structural-differences-between-men-and-women/.

16. Christian Jarrett, "Getting in a Tangle Over Men's and Women's Brain Wiring," *Wired*, December 4, 2013, https://www.wired.com/2013/12/getting-in-a-tangle-over-men-and-womens-brain-wiring/.

17. Job 2:11–13, 6:14–27, 19:21–22, 42:7–9.

18. Acts 15:3–16:10.

19. Luke 22:47–62.

20. Tim Chaffey, "Unity of the Bible: Seven Compelling Evidences," *Answers Magazine,* April 1, 2011, https://answersingenesis.org/the-word-of-god/3-unity-of-the-bible/.

Through its various outreaches and the teaching ministry of Nancy DeMoss Wolgemuth, *Revive Our Hearts* is calling women around the world to freedom, fullness, and fruitfulness in Christ.

Offering sound, biblical teaching and encouragement for women through . . .

Books & Resources Nancy's books, True Woman Books, and a wide range of audio/video

Broadcasting Two daily, nationally syndicated broadcasts (*Revive Our Hearts* and *Seeking Him*) reaching over one million listeners a week

Events & Training True Woman Conferences and events designed to equip women's ministry leaders and pastors' wives

Internet ReviveOurHearts.com, TrueWoman.com, and LiesYoungWomenBelieve.com; daily blogs, and a large, searchable collection of electronic resources for women in every season of life

Believing God for a grassroots movement of authentic revival and biblical womanhood . . .

Encouraging women to:

- Discover and embrace God's design and mission for their lives.
- Reflect the beauty and heart of Jesus Christ to their world.
- Intentionally pass on the baton of truth to the next generation.
- Pray earnestly for an outpouring of God's Spirit in their families, churches, nation, and world.

For more resources and events for tween girls, go to

MYTRUEGIRL.COM